Dance Because You Can

5 STEPS TO TRANSFORM TRAUMA INTO TRIUMPH

Outskirts Press, Inc.
http://www.outskirtspress.com

ISBN: 978-1-4787-9885-9

Library of Congress Control Number: 2018905167

Cover Photo © 2018 Amy Jordan. All rights reserved - used with permission.

Outskirts Press and the "OP" logo are trademarks belonging to Outskirts Press, Inc.

PRINTED IN THE UNITED STATES OF AMERICA

DEDICATION

This book is for you. I know how you feel. I understand your struggle. It is real.

I know you can breakthrough anything. If I did it, so can you.

I had a lot of support.

This book is in homage to those who literally saved my life, physically, emotionally and spiritually. Thank you to my dad and family.

Thank you Jennifer Lill Brown for your brilliant editing.

There are too many of you to name in person but you know who you are.

I want to give a special dedication to the late Dr. Dean Lorich. Dr. Lorich, every step I take is in your honor.

An equally special note to the William Randolph Hearst Burn Center at New York Presbyterian Weill Cornell Medical Center and The Hospital for Special Surgery along with my surgical Dream Team: Dr. Palmer Bessey, Dr. Austin Fragomen, Dr. Barry Hartman, the late Dr. Dean Lorich, Dr. Anil Ranawat, Dr. Aaron Schulman, Dr. Jason Spector, Dr. Hooman Yaghoobzadeh, Dr. Roger Yurt. Also Dr Ann Cohen, and Andy Carboy.

I cannot express in words my gratitude to Janet Horn Miller. Janet, you introduced me to the SGI USA and the practice of SGI Buddhism and chanting Nam Myoho Renge Kyo.

I truly owe you my life.

And, last but not least, my mentor in life whose heart and soul has been with and continues to be with me: SGI President and Global Scholar, Dr. Daisaku Ikeda.

With all my heart,

Amy Jordan

In Loving Memory of my Father
Dr. Robert Baum
September 12, 1931-August 14, 2018

Beautiful People!

As a visually impaired person there are many books difficult for me to read due to the text layout.

You may notice an enlarged text or more line space. This is so others with vision impairment, like myself, can easily read the print.

Thank you all and ENJOY!

Amy Jordan

Table of Contents

INTRODUCTION
Setting the Stage

HAVE YOU EVER HAD one of those moments when you think, "How could things get any worse?"

Maybe something happened and you instantly knew life would never be the same. From a divorce to a financial crisis to a health challenge to some unforeseen traumatic event, there is no shortage of things that could go wrong in this life.

I may not know you personally yet, but I do know this: We've all faced roadblocks. We've all faced tragedy. We've all been broken. We've all wondered, "How could this happen to me?"

First, let me say, "Welcome to the club."

Second, let me affirm, "You are not alone."

It may feel like you are alone right now or have been alone during those experiences in life that rock us to our core, but I'm telling you, you are not.

Would you also believe me if I told you that embedded within those difficult, seemingly impossible and impassable experiences lies the pathway to your biggest success in life?

My name is Amy Jordan, and I am here to share with you that this hidden pathway exists, and you *can* find it. How do I know? Because my greatest success in life was born out of my greatest tragedy.

The War of Two Identities

I am a dancer—and I have been since I took my first steps as a little girl. I guess it's in my DNA. I discovered the joy of dancing as a child and never looked back.

Unfortunately, a less pleasant discovery also awaited me at a young age. When I was four years old, I was diagnosed with type 1 diabetes. Growing up with type 1 diabetes was not easy. This was especially true for a kid growing up in the 1970s and 1980s. Back then, without the internet, there was no awareness of the seriousness of the disease. There also wasn't enough research to assure children with type 1 diabetes and their parents that they didn't do something wrong.

It also wasn't easy to test your blood glucose levels like it is today. I wish I could simply use a quick and simple blood glucose-testing meter. I had to stop what I was doing and go pee in a cup every single time I needed to check my blood glucose.

Making a hard situation harder, my parents chose denial as a means of coping. They did not discuss my condition. I was left feeling isolated, weird, and sick all the time. I hated that my mom had to come everywhere with me and bring along that stupid box of snacks.

I wanted to feel normal. I also wanted to eat sweets and candy like the other kids. So I began sneaking them. This secret, dangerous obsession started me down the path of developing an eating disorder that would plague me throughout my life. I wanted to eat what I wanted to eat, but the diabetes had other ideas. I chose bulimia as my way of having my cake and eating it, too.

Through it all, dance was there. Whenever I needed a

pick-me-up, dance would save the day. It became both my escape and my identity. It also provided me with an outlet for expressing myself and acquiring discipline. Dance has been my savior, time and time again.

Despite this love, I always feared that these two labels in my life—*dancer* and *diabetic*—would go to war one day. Sadly, I was right. In my early twenties, I was in Los Angeles, California, doing something that so many people never do: I was living my dream! I was dancing professionally with choreographers who worked with the likes of Michael Jackson, Madonna, and Paula Abdul.

My dreams were finally becoming reality, but then reality became a nightmare.

As a result of my eating disorder and an overall lack of attention to my health, I had drastic complications with my diabetes. After forty eye surgeries, I had to stop driving and was declared legally blind. I was in and out of hospitals, and my budding dance career ground to a screeching halt.

It was time to stop and regroup. This wasn't the first time I had to do this. My life has been filled with events that knock me down and force me to make a choice: to either stay down and give up or stand back up and keep moving forward. As a naïve twenty-something, I didn't realize that the decision to press on, time and time again, helped me develop critical life skills that would prove to be instrumental many years down the road.

Fast forward to 2009. I was living in New York and starting to find my place in the dance world again as a choreographer and producer. I was teetering on forty and terrified that crossing that age threshold would render it impossible for me to leave a legacy. This made me more determined than ever to press on. Once again, life was about to remind me that its chosen path and the one we envision are rarely, if ever, the same.

Pinned Under WHAT?

Friday, May 1, 2009, was a beautiful spring day in New York City. After a long, harsh winter, the warm sun and gentle breezes of springtime can be a literal and figurative breath of fresh air. The promise of spring revives your body and soul. It's as if suddenly everyone is happier and life seems better.

I was heading back to my office in a fabulous mood. I had been helping to choreograph and produce a performance for New York City Dance Week, and the return trip was just a few blocks. It was a journey I had made so many times, since New Yorkers tend to walk everywhere.

On this sunny, delightful afternoon, I was in no particular hurry, which is unusual for anyone on the streets of New York. I even turned off my phone and put it in my pocket, content to unplug for a few moments and soak in the rays.

I neared a crosswalk, stepped up to the curb, and looked both ways. That's what our parents taught us to do, right? I checked and saw I had the walk sign. It was my turn, and off I went.

Life is funny. Literally in the blink of an eye or the snap of your fingers, your life may never be the same. No warning. No signs. No time to prepare. Just—BAM!

In one moment, I was a girl pursuing her deferred dreams and soaking in the sun.

In the next moment, I was face down on a busy city street.

I couldn't move. I felt stuck to the ground. I also couldn't feel my right leg.

Minutes passed as I was in and out of consciousness. The sun felt warm, but the pavement felt cold. A brief springtime rain shower had left a layer of dampness on the ground, and I remember feeling dirty as I lay there in the middle of the road. I wanted to stand up and wash off all the grime, but something was holding me down.

Suddenly the need to sleep was overwhelming. In that moment, the damp New York City pavement felt like my bed. *Maybe I should take a quick nap, and when I wake up, I'll be able to move.*

A muffled voice jolted me back down to earth.

"Ma'am! Ma'am! Can you hear me?"

"Huh? What?" I abruptly replied, irritated that someone was disturbing my nap.

"Ma'am, do you know what day it is? Do you know how old you are? Who is the president of the United States?"

"President? Who cares about the president?"

"I am a paramedic. My partner and I will take care of you."

"Huh? What?" I asked again.

"Don't move!" he commanded. "We need to pull you out from under the tire of this bus."

"Under the tire? What tire? What bus?"

It seems everyone knew something I didn't. What was the big mystery? What happened is something you only see in movies. It's some mythical worst-case scenario that only exists in clichéd reminders to always wear clean underwear.

While walking across a crosswalk on a downtown city street, I had been hit. Not by a bike or a car, though. All 124 pounds of my body was pinned under the tire of a fifteen-ton New York City express bus.

I had literally been hit by a bus.

"Stay still and calm," the paramedic continued.

"Well, if I'm pinned under the tire of a bus, I don't think I'm going anywhere."

As the reality of my situation hit, I instantly felt in my heart that I would never dance again. Choreography, the shows, my dancing—it was all over.

I had no feeling in my right leg, and I wondered if it was still attached. I also sensed I was close to death. Consciousness came and went like ocean tides. Somehow, those paramedics were able to get me out from under the gargantuan tire and into an ambulance, still breathing.

On the way to the hospital, I was too scared to ask if my leg was there. I couldn't have asked the paramedics even if I wanted to after they placed a thick, suffocating collar on my neck to prevent spinal cord damage.

One minute I was living my dream; the next I felt my dreams were over. Then, just a few minutes later, when I could have easily allowed my spirit to slip away, a strange thought came to me.

I found myself chanting two words aloud over and over again: "Victory Dance . . . Victory Dance . . . Victory Dance."

The paramedics must have thought I was hallucinating, but I had never had such a clear vision of anything in my entire life.

Not knowing whether I was paralyzed, believing my right leg might be gone, and unsure whether I'd survive the night, I made a vow.

If I survived, somehow, some way, there would be a Victory Dance.

Just because You Can

Odds are you have never been pinned under the tire of a fifteen-ton bus—but have you ever faced a struggle? Have you ever encountered an insurmountable obstacle? I imagine there is something in your life that has made you feel pinned down and helpless, with no hope in sight. Now imagine taking your biggest struggle and turning it your biggest strength.

You can! All you need to do is create your Victory Dance.

How do you create your Victory Dance? That's what this book is all about.

I am a professional choreographer. My job is to tell a story by putting dance steps in a succinct order that makes sense and conveys emotion, feeling, and passion. Together, you and I will move through the five steps of DANCE, and I will show you how the hardest, most challenging events in life can create unreal and unbelievable victory. Your Victory Dance includes the following five steps:

Determination

Acceptance

Never Give Up

Courage

Enthusiasm

Creating the five steps to your Victory Dance is much the same as crafting the steps for any dance. You come up with specific moves and then put them in the order that tells the story you want to convey. Learning the steps may feel strange, or you may have challenges executing certain moves. And yet, with time and intention, the steps become normal, innate, and solid.

The process of building a Victory Dance is no different. It may seem strange or uncomfortable in the beginning. People may not respond as you thought they would, or you may slide back into old habits. The process will test all your limits—physical, emotional, spiritual, financial, and mental.

As my Victory Dance came together, the experience gave me the opportunity to examine my life up to the present and ask: *What do I really want for my future? What do I deserve?* I found that I want MORE. I deserve to live out my dreams until the day I die! That is no cliché for me.

But with so many obstacles standing in our way, how do we get there? It starts by realizing that in those moments when life tries to defeat us, we have little to no control over what happens *to* us. We do have total and complete control over how we *react* to what happens to us.

Through my own reactions and counteractions, I have created victory. Now I want to help you learn how to bridge the gap between the tragedy and the triumph.

Fortunately, you don't have to be hit by a bus to learn this dance. Everything is relative—and whatever it is that you find yourself pinned under, you can climb out victorious on the other side.

Thank you for picking up this book. I am honored that you would spend some of your valuable time reading my words to you. It is my sincere hope that moving through these steps will bring you tremendous value, beneficial information, and most importantly, JOY.

I am thrilled that we get to do this together.

It's time to start dancing just because we can!

Step One
Determination

CHAPTER 1
Making My Own Decisions

THINK OF THE BIGGEST obstacle, task, or crisis you've ever faced. Maybe it's already in the past, or maybe you're experiencing it right now. Do you feel overwhelmed? Angry? Do you doubt that you've got what it takes to get through it? I can relate. It can be debilitating to stare down that long road ahead. As scary as it can be, I have found that it helps to approach those big things in life in the same way you choreograph a dance.

A dance is quite literally just one step at a time, put in a coherent order. This is a comforting thought to me. *One step at a time. That's all. I can take one step.*

The choreography doesn't have to be completely figured out in the beginning. You figure out one move, and that leads to the next one. Sometimes you end up with a completely different dance than what you started out thinking you'd create, but most of the time, it's an improvement.

This idea helped me overcome a real-life nightmare, and now I get to share it with you and help you choreograph your *own* Victory Dance. That's an honor I do not take lightly.

Step One of the Victory Dance starts with **determination**, which is something I've always had but never recognized until later in life. You may not be sure whether you have the kind of determination it takes to wade through the worst that life can throw at you. I believe you do—and if you are holding this book in your hands right now, that means you haven't given up. That's all it takes to start moving forward!

Determine, for today, to take one more step. You can worry about tomorrow later. For now, determine to finish the day and take on your fears without throwing in the towel. We don't have the luxury of picking the hardships we experience. If we did, I certainly wouldn't have picked being crushed by a mass transit vehicle. But here's the thing—the trial itself doesn't matter. We are all blindsided by things in life. What matters is how you react to them. So let's continue my story and see what happened after my unexpected confrontation with a New York City bus.

Dr. Know-It-All

At 1 a.m. on the morning after the accident, trauma doctors performed emergency surgery to save my life and attempt to keep what was left of my leg attached. I was thankful I survived the night, but ten days later, after countless blood transfusions and numerous operations, my surgical team found themselves at a crossroads.

Simply put, they didn't know what to do with me. I became the quintessential red headed stepchild that no one wanted to deal with. Most of them blankly stared at my mangled leg and seemed completely unsure of which direction to go.

I was in bad shape. There was no skin on my leg from the ankle to the inner thigh. In many places, you could see all the way through to the bone. There were tubes and drains coming out of me at every angle. They surgically implanted an external fixator, which was essentially scaffolding for my leg that held my shattered bones together.

There I was on Sunday morning, May 10, 2009, in the orthopedic unit of a city hospital, with no answers and no real prognosis. That morning a surgical resident I like to call Dr. Know-It-All entered my room. There are people who brighten a room when they arrive, and there are those who brighten a room when they leave. Dr. Know-It-All sucked the life right out of my room every time he walked in.

On this particular morning, he pulled up a chair and took a deep breath. In an arrogant, nonnegotiable tone he looked right through me and stated, "Ms. Jordan, we are not going to be able to save your leg. You have type 1 diabetes, and your injury is too severe. We are ready to amputate above your knee."

I didn't respond, but in my mind I started screaming, *I am taking control of my own life. Not you!* Even in my drug-induced stupor, I knew it was time to take a stand and determine **not** to let them take my leg. I determined to find a better solution and to fight not just for my leg, but also for my life.

I demanded a second opinion. I would not take no for an answer.

There's Always a Better Way

The second, third, and fourth opinions of other doctors came and went, and they all echoed Dr. Know-It-All's conclusion. I remember calling a friend and sobbing, "They want to amputate. I won't let them."

In my gut, I *knew* that amputation was not the answer. I also felt that this hospital did not have staff experienced enough to treat a trauma as severe as mine —and that was before you factored in my diabetes, which only complicated things further.

Still in shock, hooked up to IVs, and receiving blood transfusions, I mobilized my community to help find the best treatment plan. I asked everyone I knew. I called my dad, other doctors, and anybody else willing to find a trauma specialist who could think outside the box.

My dad put in an emergency call to my eye doctor, Dr. Richard Braunstein. Since being diagnosed with type 1 diabetes at age four, I had experienced many devastating complications of the disease. In my early twenties, the harmful combination of denial, binge eating, and bulimia had left me legally blind after forty eye surgeries. Dr. Braunstein was the doctor who treated me after my return to New York City and helped save my sight.

Dr. Braunstein gave my dad the number for Dr. Jason Spector, who was a highly respected surgeon in the area of trauma plastics. Bright and early on Monday morning, I called Dr. Spector's answering service and explained that I been run over by a bus, had type 1 diabetes, and was about to have my leg amputated by an inept team of doctors.

Moments later my phone rang. It was Dr. Spector. In a brief conversation, I explained the severity of my situation and pleaded with him to get me out of this hospital before they amputated my leg or killed me. Ever the director, I even told Dr. Sector I would handle the transfer paperwork.

As a result, just forty-eight hours after the first hospital had declared the only answer was to lop off my leg, I was transferred to one of the best trauma hospitals in the world, New York Presbyterian Weill Cornell Medical Center, to approach my recovery in an entirely different way.

I did not accept the easy answer. I did not become anyone's victim.

As a result, I had determined my victory.

In Good Hands

On Tuesday, May 12, 2009, I arrived at the William Randolph Hearst Burn Center at the New York Presbyterian Weill Cornell

Medical Center. The burn center is a specialized intensive care unit (ICU) and not a place you ever want to find yourself. A team of nurses greeted me with open arms. It was immediately clear that these people knew how to handle serious situations and complex cases. They watched over the tiniest detail to ensure I was given the best care and the best chance for recovery.

For example, at the city hospital, I had a room full of flowers. A friend who brought flowers to the Burn Center ICU the first night was immediately told, "Sorry, no flowers here." I did not know that being exposed to pollen and other plant airborne properties was extremely dangerous for a person with no skin on her leg—and apparently neither did the other hospital.

In the city hospital, I shared a room with another patient, but now I had my own room with my own team of nurses assigned to my care. I awoke my first morning in my new surroundings disoriented and in excruciating pain, and a team of nurses and doctors quickly assembled around my bed to assist me.

At the other hospital, I had to plead for a blood glucose test to monitor my diabetes. My new nurses started testing me every hour and put me on an insulin drip along with my other IVs.

The first doctor who came to see me was Dr. Yurt. He was the polar opposite of Dr. Know-It-All. I also later found out that he is one of the most respected burn surgeons in the world. As he hovered over my leg that was being held together by scaffolding, he remarked, "You are pretty banged up."

I nodded as the painkillers lulled me back to sleep.

Despite the obvious severity of my injuries, I remember feeling an overwhelming sense of relief that I might *actually* survive. I had no idea what lay ahead, but at least I knew I was in the right place.

That second opinion saved my life.

Whenever we experience some kind of trauma or tragedy, there seems to be no shortage of people telling us which way

is the "right" choice. You can choose to listen to the wisdom and advice of others, but when it comes down to it, don't be afraid to blaze your own path.

Do you need a second opinion right now? If your gut is telling you to fight when no one else is, then go with your gut. Are you making your own decisions or is your Dr. Know-It-All making them for you? If you want control of your life, *determine* to take it!

CHAPTER 2
No One Said It Would Be Easy

IF YOU HAVE CHILDREN or were once one yourself, no doubt you are familiar with that poor, unlucky egg, Humpty Dumpty. Do you remember how the poem goes? Let's all say it together:

> "Humpty Dumpty sat on a wall.
> Humpty Dumpty had a great fall.
> All the king's horses and all the king's men,
> Couldn't put Humpty together again."

Have you ever looked like Humpty Dumpty? I think it's safe to say that most people haven't. Well I have! My leg had been broken into so many pieces that it seemed it would never fit back together again.

My friends lovingly called me Humpty Dumpty for obvious reasons. I am grateful to say that in my case, "All the king's horses and all the king's men" were some of the best trauma surgeons on the planet who attempted to make the impossible possible.

If you are facing something impossible right now, I'm not here to tell you that "everything's going to be all right." I have found that it is only going to "be all right" if you *determine* that it will be.

I didn't sit back and let fate take its course while I blindly believed that everything would work out. If you want to create your Victory Dance, it takes more than that. First and foremost, it takes determination to take control.

Luckily for me, I wasn't the only one who was determined to save me. A team of talented doctors was hell-bent on solving the seemingly unsolvable puzzle that was my shattered leg.

The Seeds of Doubt

My extended stay in the Burn Center began with surgery every four to five days for the first five weeks. At one point my sister asked one of my doctors, Dr. Bessey, how dangerous it was to perform so many major surgeries in such a short time span. He shrugged and responded, "We don't have much choice."

By now I had met the famous Dr. Spector, the man responsible for transferring me out of the city hospital. He was part of a nine-surgeon team that literally rebuilt my leg over the course of what became eighteen surgeries, some of them as long as twelve to fifteen hours each.

First, they put my bones back together using three plates and sixteen screws. I remember having a brief moment of consciousness after that extensive procedure. I reached for the external fixator that had been surgically implanted on the night of the accident. When I felt it was gone, I actually thought to myself, *Great, I'll be heading home soon.*

The next step was removing muscles from my back and shoulder and transplanting them into my right leg to replace the destroyed nerves and muscles. They then repaired my Achilles tendon and took skin from my left leg, hips, abdomen, and scalp. The new skin was then grafted onto my right leg from my ankle up to my inner thigh.

That was just the beginning of some of the hardest parts of my recovery.

After this series of major surgeries, I was assigned three amazing burn physical therapists. On the day we met, my therapist sat down in a chair next to me and smiled sweetly, as I lay there unable to move. "You are a dancer," she said. "You are going to get through this."

I shrugged, determined to believe her, even if I didn't at that moment. She didn't waste much time. With the pep talk portion of therapy quickly over, the work was about to commence. "Now let's bend your knee," she instructed.

I was not convinced I would ever walk again, so why bother? Why waste her time and mine? But I'm a chronic people pleaser, so I obliged.

Not long after we began our therapy, the same therapist came in with a walker. "Time to try standing up!"

My heart sank, tears flooded my eyes, and I swallowed hard to hold them back. Up to this point, I had not allowed the doubts to fully manifest themselves, but it was becoming harder to see the light at the end of the tunnel. The pain was too great, and the journey seemed too exhausting.

I lay motionless, unwilling to acknowledge her. It was her job to not be deterred. She unfolded the walker and stood at my bedside. "You have to get up and move."

Who would have thought that swinging a leg out of bed and trying to stand would be such a terrifying task? When you have a leg full of metal plates and fresh skin grafts, moving in any direction becomes a workout. On top of that, since a significant portion of my left back muscle had been transplanted into my leg, I had tubes and drains in my back that made moving even more difficult.

Don't try this at home, kids. It takes professionals to make it happen. But I had to try.

One Small Step at a Time

The routine was that my therapist helped me maneuver my legs until I was finally sitting upright at the edge of the bed. This was the first time I had sat up since the accident! She pulled the walker closer and placed my hands on the handles. "Put your left leg on the floor."

I wasn't so sure about this. My left leg, the good one, wasn't feeling much better than the mangled one. My left ankle had been badly sprained upon impact, and it was still incredibly sore and weak. I imagined myself crumpling into a ball on the floor, with my leg unable to support the weight of the metal plates.

Fortunately, my overachieving nature took over at that moment. I took a deep breath and sat up as straight as I could. "On three," she said as she gripped my right arm.

I made it mostly up and fell back onto the bed. Feeling slightly defeated and amazed at how difficult this task was of standing up, I decided to try again.

"On three," she repeated.

Again I pressed my hands onto the walker, took a deep breath, and pushed with all my might to stand on my left leg. With my therapist holding tight onto my right arm, I found myself upright and completely woozy. I felt like I had just run the New York City Marathon.

I was scared to breathe or move. I was terrified that I would fall or faint. Walking was this new and unfamiliar sensation. I was once so strong. *How could this happen? Is this how my life would be from now on?*

"Press your arms into the walker, push it forward, and move your left leg forward an inch or two," she directed. A sharp shooting pain radiated from the drains in my back and a sharper, indescribable pain shot out from my fresh skin grafts and permeated my entire body.

I pushed the walker barely an inch, hoisted my upper body with some help and moved my left leg, aching ankle and all. I thought I would pass out.

"You are doing great," my therapist said.

No I'm not, I thought.

"Let's do it again."

"I can't."

"Just to the door," she insisted. "Yes you can."

Holding back tears and terrified beyond words, I pushed my hands into the walker and tried to move another inch. The pain was too much to bear. Tears began streaming down my face. She knew I had reached my limit. "That's enough for today."

My friendly taskmaster came in the next morning to say, "Hello," and she also let me know that we were going to keep moving that afternoon. I said nothing. After lunch, she returned with the walker as promised. Surprisingly, I was able to stand again, and this time, we made it all the way to the door. I couldn't believe it.

I am standing!

My therapist pulled up a chair so I could rest before making the journey back to the bed. After what seemed like not nearly enough of a break, it was time to return to my bed. I hoisted my weight on my arms and moved my left leg forward. We made it the eight feet back to where we had started.

I didn't know whether to laugh or cry. *I did it!* That was the last thought I had before passing out from the exhaustion after traveling the longest sixteen feet in history.

We repeated this exercise every day. She would move my legs over the bed, place my hands on the walker, hold my right arm, and count. Then I'd inch forward on my left leg, one labored step at a time. It was way too soon after surgery to try out my right leg, but at least for now, I had conquered standing.

The decision to take control and start moving in the right

direction was not an easy one. I fought through the doubt and the pain and did the work. I was not sure I would ever dance or even walk again, but I did know that I wasn't going to let someone else decide my future.

Remember that a dance is simply one step at a time. I had taken the first steps—and although it didn't look like it to anyone around me, I was already starting to choreograph my Victory Dance.

CHAPTER 3
Face Your Fear and Win

HAVE YOU EVER NOTICED how adversity can reveal things about yourself that you never knew? If you have ever experienced the loss of a loved one, for example, you may not have realized how much that loss would affect your ability to function. Perhaps you shut down and weren't able to find the start button again for a long time, or still haven't.

Or maybe you always considered yourself to be a panic-prone person, but in a truly terrifying moment, your own bravery surprised you.

Life has a way of exposing these insights without our permission. We never ask for them or seek them out, but we receive them anyway.

What is your gut reaction to hardship? Your response in those instances—along with the actions you take afterward—will reveal what's really inside. Vince Lombardi put it this way: "Adversity doesn't build character; it reveals it."

Two Amy's: One Huge Problem

Adversity has been revealing my character for as long as I

can remember, ever since I was diagnosed with type 1 diabetes as a little girl. And the tests just kept coming.

Growing up with diabetes was a challenge. So much about my childhood felt forced and awkward, and I longed to be free of the "sick" label and achieve the greatness that I knew lived inside me.

After high school, I escaped my hometown and fled to the Big Apple, ready to go full force after what I wanted (or thought I wanted) for my life. I was in such a mad dash to "make it" that I chased whatever breeze blew past me in my pursuit of being a professional dancer. I felt all this frantic activity and dream chasing would make up for being me: sick and different.

After only a short time in New York, I decided that Los Angeles was where I really needed to be. On a whim, and with no thought whatsoever to the decision, I dropped out of college, left the professional New York City dance school where I was training, and moved to Los Angeles.

I quickly threw myself into a community of dancers who were already working with some of the biggest stars in the business. I was completely and totally intimidated, but I kept up a strong front and hid my misgivings from the world.

There was, however, one small issue holding me back—and, as it turns out, that issue was me. On one hand, I wanted to win so badly, but on the other hand, part of me never really believed it would happen. As a result, there were two Amy's at odds in my head. There was Dancer Amy—she was strong and worked hard to perfect her technical skills. Then there was Disorder Amy—she would expect to fail, self-sabotage, binge eat, and purge after feeling the shame and discomfort of overindulging.

Disorder Amy eventually began to take over both of my outward identities, and I found myself putting on a significant amount of weight in an industry in which weight gain was a career killer. My weight served as the perfect excuse to derail my success, an act I shamefully engaged in for much of my adult life.

I longed to be one of those dancers on stage with the likes of Janet Jackson, Madonna, and Paula Abdul. I wanted it so badly, and yet deep down, Disorder Amy had convinced me that it would never happen. The voices in my head were strong: *You are not good enough. You are too fat. You don't deserve to succeed.* My outward response was to keep binging.

I was caught in a vicious cycle that would only lead to destruction. I knew that mixing an eating disorder with type 1 diabetes was essentially the Molotov cocktail of lifestyle choices, but I kept going down that dangerous path.

My unhealthy choices began to manifest themselves in very real ways. I remember sitting on the pink carpet in the two-bedroom apartment I was sharing with my brother and his friend Michael in LA. I blinked hard several times, but the spots that had suddenly appeared did not go away.

That's weird, I thought. I called my father, who just happened to be a practicing ophthalmologist, and told him about these spots that had magically manifested themselves before my eyes. He demanded that I see a specialist immediately.

The next day I found myself at the UCLA Jules Stein Eye Institute under the care of Dr. Marc Yoshizumi, a world-renowned retinal specialist. He informed me I had a severe condition called diabetic retinopathy, which causes bleeding in the back of the eye due to prolonged, elevated blood sugar.

He asked me how I managed my diabetes, undoubtedly already knowing the answer.

"I manage it well," I lied. Who did I think I was fooling?

The diabetic retinopathy was fairly advanced and required extensive treatment. To address this debilitating and life-threatening disease, I had forty surgeries over the next twenty-eight months. In the end, I was left with one eye completely blind and the other eye impaired.

Despite this prognosis, I still could not control my binging and purging. Dr. Yoshizumi became so frustrated with my lack of control that he flat out told me I'd be totally blind and possibly dead within a year if I didn't get a handle on my destructive behavior.

My environment was sending me loud messages, and they were crystal clear: get help and get a handle on my life now, or lose it. All of it.

Message Received

So there I was, at a fork in the road. One path led to an abrupt dead end. The other was uncertain, but at least continued. From an outsider's perspective, the decision probably looked so clear—but anyone who has ever struggled with an eating disorder, deep-seated insecurities, or self-sabotaging tendencies knows that it's hard to see things objectively when we're neck deep in our own mess.

My left eye was completely blind and I had tunnel vision in the right. I had to stop driving. My freedom had been stolen, and I was the thief. I became bitter and felt I could never forgive myself for destroying my own life.

Despite all of this, I was somehow determined not to be defeated. I also decided I needed to take the spotlight off my failures and find more worthy ways to spend my time and energy. I soon became completely consumed with helping kids with diabetes avoid the damaging effects of mismanaging their disease.

Once I relocated from Hollywood to Santa Monica (an area that was easier to navigate without a car), I finished college and created an advocacy and outreach program called The SWEET ENUFF Movement, a nonprofit organization supporting youth with diabetes.

It was at this time when I first learned I was amazingly resourceful and courageous. I dove in without the tiniest dip of my toe in the water and boldly went for what I wanted. I knew nothing about business, but I had a vision and a mission. I would not be deterred.

Then in 1999, my friend Janet introduced something to me that would alter my path forever—the practice of SGI Nichiren Buddhism. It all started when she suggested that I chant the phrase, "Nam Myoho Renge Kyo" (like Tina Turner from the movie, *What's Love Got To Do With It*). This is the central mantra chanted in all forms of SGI Nichiren Buddhism that is believed to help eradicate karma, reduce suffering, find joy, and tap into the wisdom of life (www.sgi-usa.org).

I took to chanting immediately because I loved the way it felt. I didn't understand all of the teachings at first, but the people at the SGI meetings were warm and happy. Everyone kept telling me I had a huge mission for world peace.

As I began to study SGI Buddhism and read the essays of Buddhist philosopher Daisaku Ikeda, **I learned that every challenge is really a doorway to victory. It is also where I first heard the phrase "turning poison into medicine."**

From the perspective of SGI Nichiren Buddhism, inherent in all negative experiences is this profound positive potential. This means that any unfavorable situation can provide value and even be used for good. Perhaps more significantly, it is ultimately by determining to triumph over the painful circumstances that we grow as human beings.

Through a series of bad decisions, I was struggling to overcome an eating disorder and had largely lost my ability to see. My dreams of being a professional dancer were crushed.

There was nothing I could do to change what had already happened; **what I *could* change was myself. I began to understand that the key rests in how we *respond* to life's sufferings.**

We will all suffer—and as I studied more, I learned that it is the negative, painful experiences that often motivate us the most.

The process of changing poison into medicine begins once you start to change your mindset by viewing difficult experiences as opportunities to self-reflect. **Those adversities in life can also be used to strengthen and develop your greatest assets, such as kindness, courage, and compassion.** In SGI Nichiren Buddhism this process is known as human revolution.

When I first learned about these ideas, did I suddenly become happy? Absolutely not; I wasn't instantly fixed. I also didn't magically chant my eyesight back. I knew that I would be visually impaired for the rest of my life, but I determined to transform my existence and use my obstacles to create value. This idea would become a prominent philosophy in my life.

I *determined* to transform my situation, and in this case, support others through my nonprofit. I was already implementing the first of the five steps of my Victory Dance. Years later, as I lay flat on my back in the aftermath of a horrific accident, I would once again need to turn poison into medicine.

Can You Speak in September?

Spending months in the hospital is terrible on a level that is hard to describe. Despite the horror of my situation, I was always touched and encouraged by the outpouring of love and support I received from family and friends during my extended stay. Since I was not able to have actual flowers in my room, one friend brought paper flowers. She taped them to my wall and my window, and the story goes you could see my window from the street because of the red flowers taped to the inside.

My good friend and fellow SGI member, Debbie, was one of my regular visitors. One afternoon she informed me that she was helping plan the monthly SGI World Peace Prayer meeting.

It is customary at these meetings for someone to share a personal experience that will inspire others.

Debbie looked me squarely in the eyes and said, "You will share your experience at the September meeting."

It was mid-June, less than three months from the meeting, and I could barely stand with a walker. Most days I could hardly even lift my head off the pillow.

My initial thought was, *No way. That's impossible.* The more I thought about it, the more the idea filled me with a sense of purpose and resolve.

"I'll do it," I finally responded.

I determined that no matter what, I would stand up at that podium in September and share my story. I started visualizing myself on stage in front of hundreds of people. It was terrifying, but making this determination gave me something tangible to work toward. It became the fuel I needed to get better.

No matter your belief system, I believe the concept of finding value in adversity holds true. Religious or not, you have to ask yourself whether you are willing to grow through hardship, and whether you are willing to see good where you never thought you'd find anything but pain.

Try this with me: try to picture what good can come out of tragedy. Can you think of a way to go forward from this moment as a stronger, wiser, kinder, or better person?

This isn't an easy task, but consider the alternative: **you can either overcome the hardship, or you can allow it to defeat you.** Those are your only two options. **The good news is that you *never* have to accept defeat, so start to become open to what good is waiting to come out of the hardship you are facing.**

CHAPTER 4
Reality Is Harsh

AS MUCH AS I wanted to jump off my bed and make a mad dash to the podium, reality would prove to be different from my dreams of a speedy recovery. Days in the burn ICU turned into weeks, and weeks turned into months.

After what seemed like an eternity, my surgical and physical therapy teams began to discuss the next steps now that my stay was coming to an end. *Coming to an end?* I could hardly fathom living anywhere else.

It was decided I would be moved to a local, subacute rehabilitation center. This was a super fancy way of saying I was headed to a nursing home. I had just turned forty and was going to live in an old folk's facility.

When they told me, I burst into tears, even though I knew it was the right decision. I could not stand without help or use the bathroom unaided. I was unable to sit up for any length of time. I was still on massive amounts of intravenous antibiotics, and I continued to require significant wound care.

Still, a nursing home? *Does this mean there's still a chance I could die? Will I ever go home?* As I steadily worked myself into a panic, I thought about Debbie smiling at me, and I knew I had to stand at that podium in September and share my victory. Somehow it had to all work out.

New Kid on the Block

The nursing home of choice happened to be a few blocks from my apartment, which was a place I had not seen since that gorgeous Friday morning in May. Just thinking about the apartment was foreign. If I ever went home, would it even feel like home? More significantly, how was I going to rebuild a life that didn't seem like my own anymore?

The day of my transfer to the nursing home arrived. As the paramedics packed up my belongings and put me on a stretcher, my head started spinning. I felt completely disoriented, but when they brought me outside and the sun hit my face, I sensed a familiar twinge of warmth.

As I looked up at the blue sky, I realized that the last time I had done so was when I had a New York City bus tire on top of my leg.

Once I was safely tucked into my bed in my new room with my new elderly roommate, I quickly realized this was *not* the ICU. My attorney had said to me before the move, "Amy, you have been in the Ritz Carlton of hospitals. Anywhere you go from here is going to seem like the Holiday Inn."

Boy, was he right. I got the feeling we weren't in Kansas anymore. I also realized that I had become completely reliant on the ICU staff. They had helped me with every small task, but now I was going to have to start handling life on my own.

The nursing home staff looked bewildered by my presence. I was the youngest person in their facility by thirty years. They brought me a sandwich, set it down gingerly, and then backed away, as though I were some new, foreign species in the zoo, and they weren't sure what kind of food it would eat.

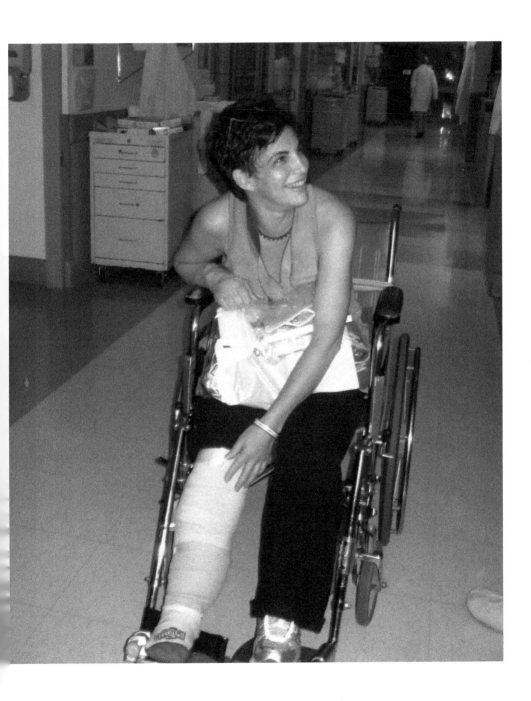

After my wound care that evening, I lay there on a plain, plastic-covered mattress in a dark room, inside the white walls of a nursing home. I could only lie on my back, and so I stared at the ceiling and felt the stark loneliness envelop me.

Internally I was reeling out of control. The move to the nursing home had brought to the surface all of the doubts I had been able to suppress during my time in the burn ICU. I had always been laser focused on my life goals, and I had finally reached a point in my life when things were clicking in the months before the accident. How did I end up here? Was "Nursing Home Amy" going to be my new identity?

This could not and would not be the end to my story.

Just One More Degree

When I awoke on day two at the nursing home, things did not appear much better in the morning light. I knew I would not be able to stomach this place for long, but I determined to improve my situation as much as I could in my present surroundings.

I quickly figured out how to get myself from my bed into my wheelchair and then into the bathroom. Who could have guessed that peeing would ever become a major life task? Making each task a little more difficult was being constantly tethered to IV lines full of antibiotics.

My feeding tube had finally been removed, but eating was a tremendous struggle due to the incessant nausea caused by the antibiotics and painkillers. Three days into my nursing home stay, I was done. I called my attorney in hysterics: "Get me out of here!"

It wasn't that simple. I could still not bear any weight on my leg, and I was too sick to care for myself or do my own wound care. So there I sat on that plastic mattress in between four sterile walls, trying not to believe this would be my fate.

The staff did their best to support my difficult medical and nutritional needs, but this was no easy task. Let's just say, for a facility with a large population of patients with diabetes, the food was ironically not diabetes friendly. After weeks of pleading, they finally allowed my friends to bring in some healthier food options.

The head nurse also helped my cause and placed me in a private room after a few weeks of nonstop requests from my lawyer. Once I had my own space, panic mode subsided somewhat, and I again resolved to get back on the path to that podium in September.

I soon got myself into a routine that seemed to work. Every day became a predictable but determined journey. The nurses came in at 6 a.m. for wound care. After they finished, I would wheel myself into the bathroom for a sponge bath. The first time I got my pants on all by myself was a truly proud moment.

Breakfast was at 7:30 a.m. After breakfast I went back to my room to chant. My occupational therapist, Chris, came in at 9:30 a.m. He was a young guy, and I could tell he was happy to have a patient closer to his age. We worked on essential skills such as getting in and out of a car, maneuvering my wheelchair through doorways, and strengthening my upper body.

Lunch was around 11:30 a.m. After lunch, I took my heavy-duty pain pills before the real physical therapy began. I was soon weaned off intravenous narcotics and given oral dilaudid, an extremely potent narcotic.

I had physical therapy every day with Rena. I chanted a few minutes before our afternoon therapy in order to gain the strength I needed to endure the pain. Rena started me out with some simple leg exercises. I say simple, but nothing was all that simple when I could barely lift my right leg a half inch off the mat.

Then came the infamous knee-bending exercise. It's a good thing I didn't know what was about to happen, because there's no way I would have let her put her hands on me had I known. Rena turned me onto my stomach, and then she took hold off my lower leg and started bending my knee. I don't have words for the pain that I felt in that moment. I sucked in as much air as I could muster and let out a bloodcurdling scream.

The daily goal during those minutes of pure torture was to get just one more degree of bend in my knee. Some days we had to stop because I was crying in agony. This little exercise became one of the most excruciating things I've ever experienced in my life.

I fought through the pain. Luckily for me, diligence and endurance paid off. My range of motion started to improve. Being in the physical therapy lab kept me focused on healing, and I was grateful for that.

Things were progressing with my therapy, and on July 27, 2009, I visited Dr. Lorich, the first surgeon to operate on me at New York Presbyterian Hospital. After a quick checkup, he asked THE question: "How would you like to try walking?" I burst into tears as he spoke these words.

No one was sure how my bones would heal or if I would ever be able to put weight on my right leg. And now, almost three months to the day of the accident, my bones had healed enough that the doctors were ready to find out. *How hard can walking be? I thought. I've been doing it since I was a baby.*

My physical therapist, Rena, did not share my rose-colored view of the process. She insisted that I not get discouraged when I wasn't up on my feet and walking right away. My right leg had literally been rebuilt. It stands to reason it may not work perfectly on the first attempt.

We started slowly. The pain pulsated up and down my body with each step. I decided to pretend it was like doing choreography and counted aloud with each grueling step.

"One, two, push walker . . . three, four, right foot forward . . .

five,six, left foot forward . . . seven, eight, stand straight."

My daily task became taking ten more steps than the day before. I had committed to stand before a large audience in just a few short weeks and share my victory. Maybe it was my ego, but I kept pushing day after day to literally take one more step.

On August 27, 2009, nearly four months to the day of the accident, I was discharged from the nursing home. With my new red walker in hand, I walked out the front door on my own two feet.

I had determined my victory and then attained it!

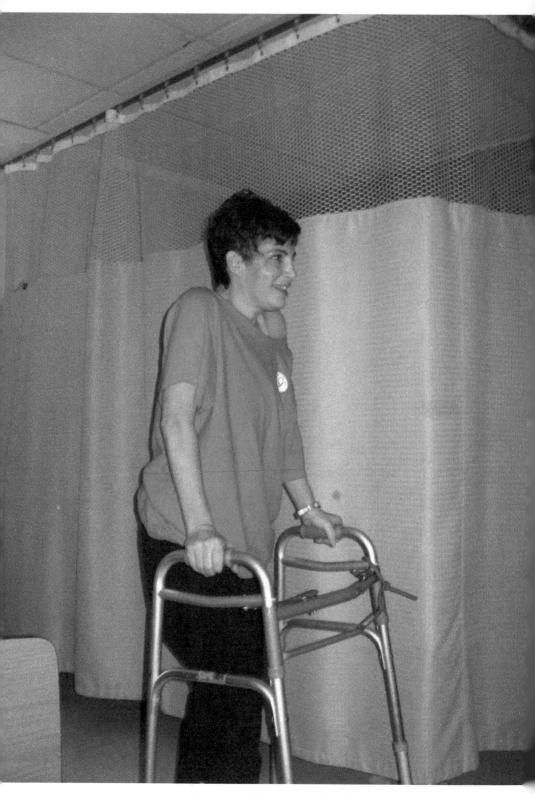

'Learning to walk again'

CHAPTER 5
Focus on the End Result

HAVE YOU EVER EXPERIENCED déjà vu?

Of course, we all know what it is—that feeling of familiarity while being in a new place. Most of the time we associate it with a weird sensation you get when you walk into a restaurant you've never frequented before, and yet it feels like you've been there before. It's also the feeling you get when you carry on a conversation with a stranger that you swear you already had.

Déjà vu is the only way I can describe the feeling that overtook me when I set foot into my apartment after months of calling a hospital room my home. When I walked in, it felt like I was seeing it for the first time. Or was I?

As I surveyed my belongings, flashes of memory came flooding back as though I were watching scenes from a movie about the life I used to have. Next to the couch sat a pile of cool-weather clothing. I remembered that on the morning of May 1, 2009, the old version of me had set them out to be folded and put away since the warm weather had finally arrived.

I had chanted and left for work from that apartment as I did every day. The old version of me had walked out of the door that morning thinking, *I really need to clean up around here this weekend.*

I also remembered feeling excited about setting new chore-ography for an upcoming show. I was living the crazy New York City life with two full-time jobs. I was also choreographing and producing on the side.

At the time of the accident, I had been involved with a man who I deeply loved. Sadly, I feared intimacy and had never been able to be vulnerable enough to tell him how I really felt. How I regretted that, because as a result we had a caring but distant connection at best. We were never quite able to commit to an actual relationship. I say "we" because I was equally terrified to let anyone get close to me.

But that had all happened to the other Amy. Now here I stood, at the doorway of my old apartment, on the precipice of a new life.

Life Goes On

My good friend Rebecca helped me to my apartment after I was discharged from the nursing home. She was one of two friends who had come to the emergency room on the night of the accident, so this was an extra big moment for both of us.

After she helped unpack my things, we decided to go for a short walk to the grocery store that was located across the street from my building. It might as well been twenty miles away. I was terrified, and I desperately clung to my new red walker as we trudged along. We made it halfway before I had to stop to rest.

When we finally arrived, I was exhausted. Now I had to shop. Everything had been done for me for the past four months. Had I forgotten how to shop? Would I be able to live on my own again?

Back in my apartment, after the harrowing journey that took

over an hour, Rebecca helped me put away my groceries. And then she left.

I sat down on the couch and stared at the wall for a few minutes. It was 7 p.m. on a Tuesday, and it was starting to grow dark outside. An unfamiliar fear—one that I had not felt since childhood—started to fill my head. I was terrified to be alone. So I did what eight-year-old Amy would have done: I walked over to my bed, crawled in, pulled the covers up way over my head, and slept with every light on in my clothes.

The next morning I took my first real shower in four months. The nursing home had arranged for a shower bench to be set up in my bathtub. I sat on the bench under the running water. *I am in MY shower!* It was a surreal moment.

Arrangements had been made for in-home wound care and physical therapy. The nurse came to change my bandages and care for my skin grafts. Then came the physical therapist for an assessment. He pushed and prodded, and we did some agonizing knee bending.

I was utterly exhausted by the end of the day. I was also desperate to gain some independence and figure out how I was going to exist in the world in my new state. I decided to walk down my block by myself and have dinner at the cafe on the corner. I asked my doorman to keep an eye on me just in case.

I got to the cafe, parked my walker, and slowly sat down at a table. A waiter came to take my order, and to my surprise, he treated me like just another normal person. I was baffled.

That's when it hit me: there were no billboards with my picture on it saying, "Watch out for this woman. She's been through a lot." The world had been going on around me, utterly oblivious to my months-long fight for survival.

I was still in excessive pain, so I decided that the pain was there to remind me that I was alive. I had collided with a bus and lived to tell the tale! And not only was I home and somewhat independent again, but I was also about to make good on a promise I had made to myself.

No Pain, No Gain

I was holding tight to the determination I had made that day on the burn unit to stand up and tell my story. It had seemed such an impossible goal, and now it was just days away.

With my leg in a large brace, I was finally able to move around my apartment without a walker. My father flew into New York City for the event, and he looked shocked when I answered the door standing up on my own, completely unaided. My sister and nephews also came to attend my victorious speaking moment. I even bought a new dress for the occasion, because why not?

Still disoriented from the pain medication, the day of the event arrived. We arrived at the SGI New York Culture Center, and I sat down with my dad in the front row. My friend Debbie asked me if I wanted to sit while speaking.

"No," I replied firmly. "I need to stand."

My moment had come. As my heart pounded out of my chest, the meeting emcee introduced me. Dad escorted me onto the stage, and I looked out over the audience of four hundred people. There were also attendees viewing the event in other rooms via live video stream.

Tears of fear and joy filled my eyes. I started fidgeting, trying to figure out how to stand on my new leg, with its deformity hidden by my long dress. The performer in me kicked in, and I began to share the unbelievable details of the previous four months. It was as if I had floated above my body and was watching someone else speak about the accident and its aftermath. As I concluded my speech and came down out of the clouds, people were standing on their feet crying, screaming my name, and clapping.

I was completely overwhelmed. Over four hundred people had just witnessed me fulfill a resolve I made in a moment when I could barely lift my head up off the pillow. I had used this determination to stay focused on getting better, learning how to walk again, getting dressed by myself, getting in and out of cars, and taking a solo shower.

I had taken Step One of my Victory Dance—and my determination was literally palpable to anyone within a mile radius of me.

I had only been discharged from a four-month hospital and nursing home stay twelve days earlier, but there I was, ready and willing to share my experience in the hopes that I might inspire just one person to climb out of his or her circumstances and take the action required to make a change.

From the moment Dr. Know-It-All decided to amputate until the moment I stood at that podium, I determined to keep

moving and step toward my Victory Dance. And what a sweet victory it was.

Jane Fonda made the phrase "No pain, no gain" famous back in the eighties in her little leotards and workout videos. I gotta say, she was right, spandex and all. The easy road would have meant less agony in the short run. The dark, lonely nights of agonizing pain I felt after an especially grueling therapy session was the stuff of nightmares. The fears that I had set my sights too high and would end up disappointed—those were almost constantly on my mind.

But I wouldn't have traded that moment standing tall behind that podium for all the pain-free days on this earth.

Easy doesn't make you grow. Easy won't get you out of the pit you may be in right now. Easy allows bitterness and regret to take root. Don't press the easy button. Determine to press on.

I'd like to say my story is "all downhill" from here. I'd love to tell you that my will to walk again got me through the hardest part of my journey. But I can't—at least not yet. There is more to this tale, and as we continue, understand that like in choreography, each step of your Victory Dance builds on the previous one.

Taking that first step is the only way to progress forward. Will you commit to determine your victory today?

Step Two
Acceptance

CHAPTER 6
Just Be Real with Me

IF YOU'VE EVER BEEN in an accident, suffered a loss, or dealt with a major failure, you can probably relate to this thought: "Just leave me alone and let me do this my way!"

As helpful as our friends and loved ones try to be, there is no universal cookie-cutter advice to follow when it comes to overcoming a painful experience. To make things more confusing, there is an endless supply of articles, books, and studies all citing the effectiveness of well-defined coping strategies in dealing with failures, setbacks, and pain.

Some work, some don't. I think it all depends on the individual. For me, one coping strategy has worked better than the rest. For many, however, it is the *one* strategy that remains the most elusive. It can be extremely hard to put into practice, but once you are able to use it, it's a mindset that can change your life for the better in so many ways. It also happens to be Step Two in your Victory Dance.

I am talking about *Acceptance*.

Acceptance is a crucial part of every Victory Dance. However, if it doesn't come as soon as you'd hoped or look like you thought it would, that's normal. When I am choreographing a work, I often create steps and then find myself totally rearranging the sequence. Ultimately it all lines up in the perfect order, like I had planned it that way from the beginning.

While the steps are being created, it is often frustrating. It can also feel like the entire process makes no sense and looks ugly when you're in the middle of it. The important part is that you keep moving forward and building the dance.

This process reminds me of a lotus flower. In SGI Buddhist symbolism, the lotus flower holds great significance. It grows in muddy water. And in fact, it is this mucky, murky environment that provides the flower's most well known meaning—the idea that when we bloom out of the darkness, this is when we achieve enlightenment.

What's even more interesting is that according to traditional stories of the flower, the more muddy and opaque the water, the more beautiful the lotus flower when it emerges. I love that! The muddier the water, the more gorgeous the flower.

I believe that your beautiful reemergence can only happen after you accept your present circumstance, however dark and murky it may be. With this idea in mind, let's keep moving forward, in the hope that your steps will rise out of the chaos and come together in a stunning, fluid rhythm.

Who Am I Fooling?

According to the dictionary, one definition of *acceptance* is "a person's assent to the reality of a situation, recognizing a process or condition (often a negative or uncomfortable situation) without attempting to change it, protest, or exit."

That seems accurate, although maybe a little academic. Let me give you my more practical take on acceptance. I believe it's the ability to look at a situation for what it is, no matter how terrible or inconvenient and think:

"This is where I am. I can't press rewind. I can accept it and choose to go forth and improve my situation, or I can choose to wallow in self-pity and resentment. I choose forward."

That is one of the toughest choices you will ever make in your life. I've had to make the choice to accept and press onward over and over again.

One of those times came not long after my move to the West coast. In 1989, I moved to LA in hot pursuit of a professional dance career, but soon after the move, I began treatment for my diabetes-related eye disease. The long-term prognosis for my sight was not good, and my dance dreams were fading along with my sight.

As a child, I wanted more than anything to be "normal," but diabetes kept that from ever being a reality. Now that I had the opportunity to follow my dreams and become a professional dancer, my diabetes complications were preventing that dream from ever becoming a reality.

It was more than just my loss of vision holding me back. At this point in my life, I was still afraid to tell anyone I had diabetes. I feared it would become my Scarlet Letter, and once people found out about it, they would shun me from their life. This made me terrified to form close relationships, become romantically involved with men, or even to date.

I knew I had to keep moving forward, dance career or not, so I enrolled in community college. My mother's voice kept ringing in my head, "You have to graduate college, and you have to marry a doctor or a lawyer."

After I started school, I found a job at a card store on the famous Sunset Strip. During my employment, I was having outpatient eye surgery on a regular basis. I was so desperate to keep this from my friends and coworkers that I even drove myself to the hospital and back for my surgeries.

Over the course of a few months, I had become good friends

with the store manager, Michael. Much to my delight, we started spending a lot of time together as friends. I had never been in a romantic relationship. Needless to say, I developed a huge crush on Michael.

The more time we spent together, the more cunning I became at hiding my condition. Michael even drove me to a few eye appointments but had no idea what was causing my vision problems. I asked him to wait in the waiting room while I met with the nurses. I was terrified they would mention my diabetes, and Michael would learn my ugly secret.

When he asked why I was having these problems, I flat out lied and said it was hereditary. I would run to the restroom to inject insulin. If I felt low blood sugar coming on, I would ever so nonchalantly sip on some juice or soda.

I thought I was fooling the world. In the end, all I was really doing was inflicting self-torture and becoming more miserable in my own skin. I couldn't tell Michael I had romantic feelings for him. I wasn't sure how he felt about me, and part of me wondered if he was gay. Unfortunately, my fear of intimacy kept me from asking the hard questions.

As I needed more eye surgery, he began to ask more questions. Because he cared about me, he started doing some old-fashioned research. This was 1990, long before Google. One evening we were sitting in the back office closing out the store for the day. I was sitting on a stool at the counter; Michael was sitting in a rolling chair at the desk.

He twirled around in the chair, wheeled to my side, and looked up at me on the stool.

"I know," he said.

Tears welled up in my eyes.

"I figured it out," he continued. "All the clues."

I put my pen down and looked at him. *What do I do now?* I thought. I was almost more ashamed of lying to him than I was of the diabetes.

"It's not a big deal," he said. "It all makes sense now."

That evening I took my insulin in front of Michael.

"Does this bother you?" I asked nervously. "I do it every day."

"I just want you to be healthy."

Michael and I never became romantic, but his purpose in my life was no less profound. Confronting me about my diabetes and not running for the hills gave me the push I needed to take my first step into acceptance.

He gave me an opportunity to be who I really was with no shame. He accepted me—Scarlett Letter and all. As a result of his acceptance I began to feel more comfortable with myself and with my diabetes. I stopped hiding in bathrooms every time I needed to take an insulin shot.

The first time I injected insulin in public was at Jerry's Deli in North Hollywood, California. Nobody even noticed. *Wow, I thought. Maybe I can stop hiding now.*

The disease itself had not changed, but what began to change was how I responded. Pretending it wasn't there had already done irreparable damage to my eyes. It had also built a wall that prevented real relationships from forming. I finally accepted my condition and began to speak more openly about having diabetes. Each time I brought it up with friends new and old, I grew more confident.

I have lost touch with Michael over the years, but I hope in some way he knows what a crucial stepping-stone he was to undertaking Step Two in my Victory Dance.

Take a moment to stop and be thankful for the people in your life, past or present, who have helped you see important truths. I am willing to bet that of all the people you have ever known, only a small handful of them changed your life for the better. I encourage you to tell those few special people how they have affected your life in a positive way. I'd love to have the opportunity to hug Michael and tell him what he accomplished in my life.

Part of the true beauty of life is that it is unpredictable. No matter how hard you try, you'll never be able to forecast the future. No matter how prepared you think you are for every imaginable scenario, you'll never be able to prepare for some of life's biggest surprises. No matter how much you would like things to stay the same or at least go back to the way they were, you'll never be able to stop change.

We can't turn back time. That is why the ability to accept whatever comes your way is not just a good idea—it's really the only way to truly live. That is also how we become like the lotus flower—by wading through the muck until we emerge victorious on the other side.

CHAPTER 7
Facing the Truth

ONE OF THE MAJOR gripes of television hospital dramas is that they are phony and unrealistic. I read an article once that said in real life, CPR saves lives just five percent of the time. But on TV, people are constantly brought back to life with some quick CPR!

TV doctors also seem to come across more high-adrenaline cases in an hour than most real doctors see in their entire career. That is why the doctors and nurses on call in the ER on May 1, 2009, must have thought they stumbled onto the set of a television drama.

"A woman was run over by a New York City bus? No freaking way!"

Here I am, putting *Gray's Anatomy* to shame with my own implausible story line. It might as well have been fictional. For the first few weeks, I felt like I was watching someone else's drama unfold. The pain was real, but that was about the only thing that kept me grounded. That is, until I met some amazing people that helped put me back on the path toward my Victory Dance.

Human beings can be amazing. They can support us when we have nothing left. They can be our voice of reason when we feel like we are going insane. Without my friends and the special people I met during this time in my life, Step Two of my Victory Dance would never have been possible.

It Looks Like Hamburger Meat

Michelle was one of those special people. She worked in the burn ICU and was frequently there with me during my daily visit to the Tank. The Tank was a series of large rooms where burn patients were taken to receive a sponge bath and get our skin grafts cleaned. On special days they even washed my hair. Sounds nice, right?

It was a house of horrors.

Michelle would come into my room and wheel my bed into the Tank where I was then transferred onto a stainless steel table. I was always given an extra high dose of painkillers prior to entering the Tank, but it was of little use. Taking pain meds before a visit to the Tank was like throwing a thimbleful of water onto a raging inferno.

Healing fresh skin grafts and regenerating nerves cause pain on a scale that can't be put into words or comprehended unless it is something you have experienced. In addition to the skin grafts, I had a serious bacterial infection, which caused the grafts to ooze and require additional cleaning.

I am a generally low key, quiet person, but in the Tank, I found myself screaming for my life. Michelle was amazing at distracting me from the pain. She chanted with me, told jokes, put on the radio and danced around me—anything to keep my focus off what was happening.

She also encouraged me to try to look at my leg. While Michelle and some of the other nursing staff had been politely suggesting that I take a look, I had yet to do so. My rational mind was fully aware that I was in the ICU and had been there for over a month, but the magnitude of what had happened to my body had not sunk in yet.

A few times a week a psychiatrist stopped in to see how I was doing.

"I am not depressed," I would reply with a Cheshire cat smile. "I will be good as new soon."

I was still in shock and denial, and my unwillingness to look at my leg wasn't helping.

My sister came down from Maryland regularly to be with me at the hospital. One day, she accompanied me into the Tank. Once all my dressings were removed, she remarked that my leg looked like "uncooked hamburger meat."

That was all I needed to hear. I wasn't interested in looking at my meat leg any time soon. I wanted to go on thinking my appendage was just as I remembered it.

My treatment team grew increasingly concerned about my lack of willingness to accept my new reality. Michelle came into my room one afternoon after my visit to the Tank. She looked at me sternly and said, "Amy, you need to look at your leg. It is important for your healing."

The extreme people pleaser in me wanted to do what she said immediately to make her happy—but even that was not enough for me to take a glimpse. I had worked really hard not to look for this long.

I could go longer.

The image I had in my mind of my old leg was good enough for me. That version was a dancer's leg. That's the one I wanted to hold on to.

It's Time, Amy

They say necessity is the mother of invention. After I was discharged from the burn ICU and arrived at the nursing home,

I had no choice but to get a glimpse of my new body.

Between the fresh, oozing skin grafts and the infection, it was a mess down there, which meant I needed highly specific wound care. When the staff came in to change my dressings and clean my wounds, they started asking me lots of questions and seemed unsure of themselves.

I realized that in order to be sure my wounds were properly dressed, I had to sit up and direct the process. The nursing home staff unwrapped my bandages. I blinked hard. *This can't be real life*, I thought. *That is NOT my leg.* Maybe I am just filming an episode of Grey's Anatomy. This can't be REAL.

My leg was swollen to four times its normal size. It was dark purple and red in color and the newly reconstructed nerves and veins were bulging under my thin new skin. The grafts were oozing all over the place. It was stomach turning. My sister was right—it really did look like raw hamburger meat. There was no "leg" shape left. It more closely resembled a gnarled, burned, sticky tree branch.

Staring at reality was one of the toughest things I had ever done. It was horrible, and yet at the same time, it was clarifying. It all made so much more sense now. I finally got why this had been so hard. I finally understood why I was still lying in a hospital bed. And I realized why Michelle kept pressing me to look at it.

For all those months, I had convinced my mind that my leg looked just like how I remembered it. Now that I knew what I was really up against, I was able to start coming to grips with what lay ahead.

If I had it to do all over again, I'm not sure I would have had the courage to look at my leg any sooner than I did. Everyone steps into acceptance according to his or her own timing. No one but YOU knows when you are ready to take that step — but at some point, it must be taken.

Your Victory Dance will never come until you are willing to accept what you see in front of you.

We need to believe that everything will "be all right." That is why it's often easier to ignore how bad, ugly, or painful things are in the present moment. The problem with that approach is that **hanging on to a false reality will only cause more disappointment, anger, and resentment down the road.**

Seeing my leg for the first time was a critical step toward acceptance. It forced me to stop thinking I was watching some TV hospital drama and face reality. Your mind really does believe whatever you tell it. Without seeing my leg, it would have been impossible for my mind to begin figuring out how to move on and turn tragedy into triumph.

Acceptance is a choice. It's a tough one but it is a choice nonetheless. If you'd like to take a step closer to creating your Victory Dance, decide to accept things as they are in the present moment and go from there. It won't instantly fix everything, but it will open up some doors you couldn't see before and give you and your loved ones the hope that one day, things really will "be all right."

CHAPTER 8
Are We Done Yet?

LOOKING AT MY LEG was a grounding experience, but I was still unable to let go of the dream that everything would soon return to normal. I was living in a fantasy world where a collision with a bus was the equivalent of a minor tumble off a bike.

You'd think all the stares on the street would have helped bring the reality home. Kids seemed especially fascinated. I lived in a building with lots of families, and the little ones would quietly ask their moms and dads what was wrong with me. In an effort not to scare the children, their parents would reply, "It's nothing, honey. A doctor just operated on her leg."

I'm not an idiot. I knew it looked bad. If I were a kid, I'd be curious, too. Even so, all the stares and questions only strengthened my resolve to get back to Normal Amy mode that much faster.

After my discharge from the hospital, my outpatient rehabilitation began, and I was determined to make the most out of every moment. I was not in denial anymore about the severity of the injury, but I was a hard worker. I felt my work ethic and resolve would be the springboard I would use to speedily rehabilitate my way back to the way things were.

My surgical team had told me that even after I was able to go home, I would require further surgery. I scoffed at this idea. *I won't need any more surgery*, I told myself.

I couldn't have been more wrong.

Amy versus Reality

When I finally returned to my apartment, I had all these grand visions of what life would be like in just a few short months. I'd play an imaginary montage in my head of me kicking ass at my rehab appointments and wowing the doctors and nurses with my miraculous recovery.

In my fantasy world, it was all coming together. In reality, my knee basically had no functioning ligaments. I also had a massive bacterial infection. Just three months after my initial discharge, I was back in surgery. A common knee procedure escalated into a severe situation thanks to the rampant infection.

The first six months of 2010 were spent in or recovering from surgery. I had multiple procedures relating to the infection in January, February, and March. Much to my dismay, the metal plates and screws holding my battered bones together were so infected they all had to be removed. Dr. Lorich stopped in to see me in the recovery room.

"Your infection was much worse than we thought," he said. "We had to remove all the metal."

"Can I walk?" I asked.

"No," he replied.

My heart sank into my chest. All my work had been for nothing. How could this be happening? My entire life was a lie. Now they say I can't walk. I shut down. In that moment I truly wanted to die. I refused to speak to anyone. I just lay there on the gurney wishing I had not survived.

Dr. Spector came in a few moments later. He noticed my

state. He reminded me that what they had done to save my leg had been nothing short of "heroic."

I still felt like I was suffocating. With more IV lines full of antibiotics I was admitted into a hospital room. In my mind it was over.

To make matters worse, I was sent back to the nursing home. It was February and one of the coldest and snowiest winters in years. I felt I was regressing with no means of recovery. My hope was running out.

After another round of IV antibiotics to treat the infection, Dr. Lorich and Dr. Spector would try a new approach.

Finally on March 17, 2010, I had a much-needed bone graft. My shinbone had been so badly damaged that it no longer had sufficient bone mass to function. Bone tissue was taken from my right hip and grafted into my leg to hopefully provide my leg with the mass it needed to support my weight.

The procedure was a success, and I was cleared to start walking again. I quickly resumed rigorous physical therapy and planned to continue as long as my insurance would allow. I had determined that by my birthday, May 31, I would be off my walker and able to walk with a crutch. It was a big task, but the thought of being a forty-one-year-old woman on a walker was more than I could take.

On my birthday, I walked down my block to a café on the corner, aided only by a crutch. That fulfilling victory was followed by a crushing blow. A few days later, Elise, my burn therapist, told me that we had reached the end of our sessions.

"How do you feel?" she asked.

I felt totally deflated. I looked at my puffy and swollen red leg. I felt the limited movement. I had envisioned that by the time my outpatient therapy was over, everything would be back to its pre-bus form.

"So that's it?" I said in disbelief. "This is it?"

She reminded me how far I had come since she treated me in the burn ICU. "You have had a serious trauma, Amy. Your leg will be functional, but it will never be what it was."

I did not respond. *No, I can't believe that. I won't believe that.*

My leg felt so strange with all its new skin, pulling in directions that skin isn't supposed to pull. My ankle felt locked in place; my knee had limited mobility. Not to mention the fact that my leg was seriously deformed. I could only wear sneakers, and even those were a challenge at times.

After our therapy session ended, I went home and pulled out all my old shoes and threw them into a bag. The next day I had a friend take all those stylish pumps and sandals I'd never be able to wear again to the thrift store.

The reality had hit home. Things would never be as they once were, and if I had left those shoes in my closet, they would have been a cruel reminder of what I once took for granted—a leg that could run, dance, and look cute in a normal pair of shoes.

Is This the End or the Beginning?

My surgical team was still battling the massive infection in my leg, and I had one final major procedure on February 12, 2012. By the end of that summer and into the next year, it seemed as if the infection was gone. I was finally free to start healing—physically and emotionally.

The lack of surgery left a strange void in my life. In some ways, being in a hospital for so long, constantly battling surgery, and attempting to overcome such immense physical obstacles was easier than tackling the hard question: *Now what?*

Dealing with all the complications had been the perfect excuse to avoid the inevitable next steps and delay true acceptance. With the final major surgery done and no more therapy, my days went from being full of appointments, rehab, poking, and prodding to a whole lot of nothing.

People would ask me what I was going to do. It made me furious.

"Gee, I don't know," I'd snap back. "I've never been run over by a bus before."

My new body was so weird. I walked with a limp. I wore a large knee brace much of the time. People stared at me constantly. While I was now able to look at my leg, it still felt like some foreign appendage. I would catch myself staring at other people's legs as they walked down the street. I also became fixated on women in cute shoes.

People were constantly telling me how inspired they were by my recovery. I smiled and said things like, "Oh, I'm so glad," but inside I *despised* those comments. I felt deformed and hopeless. I sat on my couch and stared at the ceiling, wondering why I even survived.

To be perfectly honest, I just got bored with myself. One day I got off the couch to go work out. As I got dressed I thought, *You are gonna have to figure out something else because whatever this is isn't working.*

I wish I could say I had some earth-shattering moment or big epiphany after that, but I did start to slowly figure out a few things. First, I came up with some great ways to respond to the dumb comments and questions people kept throwing at me. When they asked if I sued the city or how much I got in my settlement, I responded with, "Actually, I haven't worked in years, and I have $2 million in medical debt. Can you lend me $50 bucks?"

I started smiling directly at people who stared at me on the street. I found ways to redirect the conversation away from my accident. When people began sharing unsolicited advice, I stated that if I needed any help I would ask. I would literally put my hand up and stop them midsentence.

I felt like I was taking back control of my life. I had gone to work creating a new state of being Normal Amy. Once I began to accept my leg as my own, my life began to take some amazing turns for the better. The long process of accepting my new body and my new life had begun.

I can't say the process is over, as I am a work in progress to this day. I do know that the more I face the obstacles head on and accept them for exactly what they are, the faster they resolve. I also know that I am learning to take care of myself first. If anything, the accident taught me how to enact true self-care.

Acceptance is not a cure-all. I still had (and still have!) a long way to go. But I was starting to feel more and more like me again. I didn't know what this new version of me was going to do with her life, but I was becoming more interested in finding out.

CHAPTER 9
Yeah! Well I Don't Like Hospitals Either

I HAVE STRUGGLED WITH romantic relationships for most of my adult life. As a kid, I wore my diabetes like a badge of shame. Although I hid these feelings well as I got older, I never outgrew them.

All of my relationships with men up to that point shared some things in common: no clearly defined boundaries, no truly intimate connection, and zero honesty. I seemed incapable of letting my guard down enough to connect with people, and especially men, in any real or genuine way.

I desperately wanted a real romantic relationship. The older I got still being single the more shame I felt. I had begun to feel as if something was just wrong with me or that maybe I just had to accept I would be single forever.

I am a people pleaser, so I did my best to seem like an extrovert, but I was a closeted loner. I isolated myself as much as I could without making it too obvious, but I knew how to turn on the charm when the situation called for it.

I was my own island. I had grown accustomed to feeling this way, but it never bothered me as much as it did on May 1, 2009. As the paramedics carted me away to the hospital in the moments after my accident, they asked if I had a significant other or any family to call.

"No," I responded.

That wasn't entirely true. I had been seeing someone for several years at that point, but I knew in my heart that this man may or may not show up in this particular emergency. I did not have any family in New York City. I needed someone at my side so I had the paramedics call a fellow SGI Nichiren Buddhist friend who came to the emergency room with another friend.

In the emergency room, I had asked my friend to call Tom and tell him what happened. I hoped and prayed he would show up. A small, sentimental part of me was holding on to the fantasy that he would come running into the room, tell me how devastated and broken he would have been if he had lost me, and we'd ride off into the sunset.

Holding Tight to the Fantasy

Tom called the next day, and my heart leaped with joy. I told him I missed him and asked if he was going to come by the hospital. Looking back, I should not have even had to ask.

He responded that he did not "do hospitals."

My heart abruptly sank. He proceeded to share a story about an accident he had many years earlier. He said he was taken to the hospital, but he had signed himself out and nursed his wound himself.

"But I have no skin on my leg and my bones are crushed," I replied.

No response.

Little did I know this would be the beginning of the end of

a detrimental pattern of niceness that I would be stuck in for years. While I still strive to be a nice person today, the old version of me regularly took niceness to the "getting trampled on" level. I could never tell people how I felt or call someone out when it was appropriate. I had no boundaries and made excuses for people rather than ever dare to face any difficult situation or a confrontation.

In the coming weeks I had a room full of flowers and a flow of visitors around the clock. Sometimes people I didn't even know came to see me. Other times, I had to ask people to leave because I was too tired to put on a brave face and be polite.

My extroverted introversion was in full swing. I was terrified of everything going on around me and desperate to find someone with whom I could be real. Many fellow SGI Buddhists came to chant with me. I continued to put on a good front for them and for everyone else, always careful to hide how scared I was.

In the back of my mind I kept hoping that Tom would show up and be the rock that I needed. As days in the burn ICU turned into weeks and months, I would call Tom at all hours, often extremely high on narcotics. Every morning I woke up thinking today would be the day he would waltz in my room and hold my hand. On May 31, my fortieth birthday came and went in the burn ICU. Tom never came.

Four months after my accident and a week after my discharge from the nursing home in August 2009, Tom came to see me at my apartment.

"You look good for somebody who's been through all that," he said.

I shrugged my shoulders. My leg was in a full brace from thigh to ankle. It was still incredibly swollen, and my pink skin grafts were raw and just starting to heal.

We chatted about nothing for a while. I could sense he was

unsure of what to say. I recognize that it must have been an awkward moment for him. His life had kept going while mine had literally been squashed flat.

Finally I took off the leg brace, rolled up my pants and showed Tom my new leg. He literally turned purple. He excused himself and headed for the bathroom. I know it was a lot to take in. I probably would have walked away too.

He came back in the room somewhat composed. His color had returned. I had covered my leg back up. Wanting to be positive he started suggesting possible ideas for how I could get back to work.

"I can't climb stairs or get on a train," I said.

He stared at me with one eye while the other one eyed the door. We chatted a bit more and then he left. I felt numb.

I continued to allow Tom to be a part of my life. I know that seems insane. We had known each other a long time and while my feelings about our "relationship" were complicated there was something comforting about his visits. As strange as it may seem, the fact that he had not been through my rebuilding and just treated me like he always had helped me feel normal. The fact he was still attracted to me after everything that had happened also helped me feel less broken.

This was also the beginning of a difficult lesson in true acceptance. I wanted something from him he would not or could not give me. I can't really blame him. It was my expectation and lack of communication about my feelings that was the root of my suffering around our situation.

Supernova 2013

Have you ever seen what a star looks like when it dies?

The Hubble Space Telescope has caught a few of them in their final glorious moments. I say "moments," but it's an event that goes on for quite some time. All of that unstoppable fire and energy bursts forth in shockwaves of magnificent destruction.

I experienced my own supernova when things with Tom finally came to a dramatic and intense breaking point almost four years after my accident. The scene was so cliché. It really was something right out of a big screen melodrama.

In the aftermath of the explosion, I cried for months. I broke down physically, emotionally, and spiritually. I had put a tremendous amount of energy into our uncommitted "relationship" for a lot of selfish reasons. The most obvious reason was that it served as a much-needed distraction from what was really happening in my world.

The emotional pain seemed almost worse than the physical pain I had endured. The idea of the only hope of a relationship with a man, as dysfunctional as that connection may have been, had finally been snuffed out. I felt the kind of isolation I hadn't felt since I was a young, diabetic girl being followed around by her lunatic mom and that stupid wicker basket of snacks. My dance did not seem victorious at all.

I recognize that the entire ordeal with Tom and with the accident itself afforded me some much-needed relational housecleaning: friends, romantic, business, and family relationships. Some people were genuine, but so many others were drama magnets who were attracted to the trauma of it all.

I started attending a well-known support system for people ready to overcome and transform difficult, harmful relationships. Those meetings helped me figure out what I really wanted and needed from the people around me, in all capacities of relationships.

They say you find out who your real friends are when you are at your lowest. I definitely found this to be true. I began to take a good, hard look at who sincerely supported me through nearly sixty surgeries throughout my life, years of life-and-death challenges, a tremendous financial crisis, and intense emotional distress.

At some point in the recovery process, it became more desirable to stay home alone rather than go out and face the constant questions about my leg and my lawsuit. Being forced to hear everyone's thoughts, ideas, and feelings about my situation and what I should do with all the money I did not have was soul draining.

It seemed every time I turned around, somebody else had what a friend termed "street solutions" for my legal and financial woes. No one ever asked me what I thought about my own life. Everyone talked about how "thankful" I must feel. I was such an "inspiration" to others that I felt ashamed for feeling sorry for myself.

It has taken many years to fully unravel all that occurred between Tom and me. I had to let go of my anger. Today I truly believe it was all for the best. Every girl I know has had at least one major heartbreak in her life. It makes us stronger, and it helps us fight harder for what we deserve the next time.

I also see there were many people who came to visit me in the hospital who I have not heard from in years.

Tom and I have since been able to honestly and openly communicate about our connection and the obstacles we encountered. We are actually better friends today than we have ever been. Through my recovery I have learned how to communicate my needs without being reactive, manipulative, passive aggressive, or just crazy.

It has been a tremendous lesson in letting go of resentment and embracing forgiveness.

As a close friend has said, Tom has truly been and continues to be my great teacher.

This is not one of those situations where I'd say, "If I had to do it all over again, I wouldn't change anything." Actually,

I'd change a lot. First, I would have loved myself more. I would have also opened my mouth and asked direct questions like, "What do you want out of this relationship?" or "What are we?" or "Do you want this to work?" Any of them would have been more helpful than living in denial.

I don't recommend experiencing your own relationship supernova, but for me, it was a necessary part of figuring out how to accept my life, my body, and the role of other people in my existence. I am happy to say that since that time, Tom and I have reconnected and forgiven each other for the pain and confusion we both caused.

As time has passed, I am becoming increasingly confident in who I am as a person, and I have stopped apologizing for the goals I am working to achieve. I don't apologize for feeling down or frustrated. I have stopped caring what other people think. I also accept that I have a glorious future.

Part of taking Step Two in your Victory Dance means accepting not just your present situation, but also accepting and loving who *you* are at this present moment. I am grateful that I was given a chance to see my relationships in a clearer light. It's made me a better friend, and it's great to know that the people in my life now are there because we mutually respect and love each other! That's still a new feeling for me—and I can't believe I waited so long to experience it.

This step of the Victory Dance has been and continues to be messy for me, but it's also where the magic happens. I've lost count of the number of times I've totally changed the direction of a dance I'm choreographing. While the outcome is amazing, it always looks contorted or strange in the midst of recreating the work.

Step Two in the Victory Dance is exactly the same. It gets messy. You may cry or scream like I did and sometimes still do. You may not understand anything going on in your life, and you might feel overwhelmed. You may also feel like acceptance will never come.

Keep moving. Like choreography, the steps sort themselves out, and with acceptance comes a sense of peace and the ability to move through anything.

Step Three
Never Give Up

CHAPTER 10
You Can't Operate: I Have to Meet The First Lady.

CAN I BE BRUTALLY honest?

When people used to say to me, "Never give up!" I felt like punching them.

"How can you say this to me?" I wanted to scream. "Don't you know my life is over? At first I was just legally blind and living with diabetes, but now I'm crippled, alone, and saddled with a mind-blowing amount of debt."

Hindsight being twenty-twenty, I have to laugh at myself. While I was secretly lashing out at everyone who told me to "never give up," it is exactly what I was doing. I never gave up. I hate to admit it, but it's true.

I'm not just talking about in the months and years following the accident, but throughout my entire life. Somehow, some way, my unspoken mantra has always been NEVER EVER GIVE UP. I instinctually recognized one important truth, which was this: once you reach a dead end, the only way to find a new path is to look for it. It's not going to materialize out of thin air, and it's not going to come to you. You have to go find it!

Sometimes I go home and hide under the covers for a day or two. But I don't stay there long. Ultimately, I keep the dance going. I push forward and look for the open path, focused on the end result. The Victory Dance is exactly the same. When you feel it can't get any worse or there is no solution, keep moving. Believe it or not, the grass IS often greener on the other side.

Infection? What Infection?

By late 2011, my revolving door into the operating room was still in full swing. I was beginning to doubt whether I'd ever reach the end of the challenges, surgical corrections, and subsequent complications. However, I've never been one to sit back and "let the chips fall," so I decided to start *doing* and *acting* rather than just *being* and *reacting*.

With the help of a business partner, I revived my SWEET ENUFF Movement. The two of us tirelessly worked to create curriculums, write grants, implement programs, and network for the right board members.

Looking back, it was pretty astonishing what we accomplished with so much stacked against us. For starters, we had no money. I had not worked in years and now had millions of dollars in medical debt. I was still having surgery and trying to heal. I was regularly going to doctor visits and physical therapy sessions.

Somewhere in the midst of this flurry of emotional and physical stress and activity, my cohort and I created the SWEET ENUFF Wellness Challenge. In the spring of 2011 we interviewed and hired dance teachers and nutrition coaches, secured major school contracts, and raised enough money to keep the program going.

It just so happened that First Lady Michelle Obama had

recently taken on the youth diabetes epidemic. She had just launched her Let's Move campaign and created the Partnership for a Healthier America (PHA).

The first PHA Summit would be in Washington, DC, the week after Thanksgiving. A few weeks before the summit, I mystically received a large sum of back pay from disability. We took it as a sign that we were meant to go, and I purchased two tickets.

Unfortunately, the timing wasn't looking so good. I had major surgery in September 2011. The surgeons re-broke my right tibia in order to straighten it and pinned it externally with another external fixator, so once again my leg was encased in scaffolding. On top of this I was still battling a major bacterial infection in my bones.

On the Friday after Thanksgiving, I noticed there was a spot on my leg that was oozing yellow puss. *Oh boy,* I thought. *Here we go.* I called Dr. Fragomen, my rock star orthopedic trauma surgeon. He gave me specific instructions and said if it had not improved, I would need to see him in his office first thing Monday morning.

Monday morning? That was the same day I was supposed to leave for Washington, DC, to woo our country's First Lady. I was divided between fear and rage. Didn't anyone understand that I was working diligently to get myself back to some state of normalcy?

Monday morning arrived and the draining abscess had expanded into two draining abscesses. I called Dr. Fragomen's office, and of course, he wanted to see me immediately. I got in a taxi—suitcase and SWEET ENUFF merchandise in hand—and went to the hospital.

Dr. Fragomen came into the exam room, and before he had a chance to crush my dreams, I said, "I know this is serious, but I have to be on a train at 3 p.m. to meet the First Lady. If you have to operate, can we schedule it for Wednesday?"

Dr. Fragomen, one of the most amazing people I have ever known, took one look at my face and knew I was not kidding. He also knew the situation had to be addressed in a way that would not put my life at risk.

Surgery could wait, at least for a day or two. He drained the oozing abscesses, prescribed more antibiotics, and gave me specific instructions for draining and packing the wound. I flew out of his office at 11:45 a.m. and took a taxi across town. I had to visit two different pharmacies to get everything I needed to manage my infection. It was now close to 1 p.m.

I called my sister who lives in Maryland and asked if she could bring some wound-care supplies and meet me at the train station when I arrived. I got back to my apartment at 1:45 p.m. to pack more supplies, hailed another cab (I spent nearly 120 dollars in taxi fare that day) and zoomed to Penn Station. I made my train with ten minutes to spare, oozing leg and all.

My sister met me at Union Station in Washington, DC, and delivered the remaining supplies. I was exhausted but extremely proud of myself for not giving up. I wasn't going to let my current circumstances stop my forward movement.

Today You Are Going to Own It

My business partner and I were determined to make the most of every connection we made at the PHA Summit. We networked until I could barely stand. On the final day of the event, First Lady Michelle Obama was scheduled to give a keynote address in the hotel's main ballroom.

That morning, there was a line of people a mile long waiting to be cleared by Secret Service. My friend grabbed me by the arm and whispered, "I know you hate being labeled as disabled, but today you are going to own it."

Since we had been connecting with people during the summit, many of them knew my story and happily moved aside to let us pass. When we got to the front of the line, my tall, beautiful friend flashed the Secret Service agents a big, captivating smile.

"Excuse me," she began. "My friend is disabled and can't stand in this line."

As the Secret Service agent looked my way, I pulled up my pants leg. He gazed upon my deformed leg, the metal rod poking out of my bones, and the yellow patch on my bandage that had drained from the infection.

"Wow," was all he could muster. Needless to say, we were immediately fast tracked to the front of the line. My business partner and I were allowed into the ballroom before it even opened. Since the room was mostly empty, we sat down in the front row, smack dab in the center.

Mrs. Obama gave a poignant keynote address. She is even more radiant in person than she appeared on TV. As soon as she finished speaking, my cohort jumped out of her seat and ran toward the media partition between the stage and the audience.

The First Lady was accepting a receiving line for everyone standing at the partition, so I hobbled as quickly as I could into the line. A few moments later, there she was, First Lady Michelle Obama, standing right in front of me. She smiled a gracious, warm smile and shook my hand as I looked up at her. Wow, was she tall!

I knew I only had a few moments. First, I thanked her for her tremendous efforts for our youth. Then I briefly shared how I had become visually impaired due to mismanaged diabetes, and after forty eye surgeries was now legally blind. I told her about our mission to prevent such adversity from happening to kids who were dealing with diabetes or obesity.

We had a short yet focused exchange about the importance of the health of young people. She hugged me and again flashed that amazing smile. I turned around, and as Mrs. Obama and I were laughing, my business partner snapped the photo that is now framed and hanging on my wall.

To this day, she does not know that hidden under my pants was a crushed leg with a draining infection. Mrs. Obama did not know that forty-eight hours earlier I had commanded my trauma surgeon to patch me up so I could get on that train to Washington, DC, and meet her.

It didn't matter that she did not know. While the obstacles seemed impassable, I kept focused on the goal of getting on that train. I did not give up on my opportunity to manifest that moment with the First Lady.

Nearly two years later, in January 2013, my SWEET ENUFF Movement became a top five national finalist in the PHA's "End Childhood Obesity Challenge." When-ever I get frustrated or start feeling defeated, I look at that photo with Mrs. Obama. It is a daily reminder not to give up no matter how challenging the external circumstances.

With the amazing
First Lady Michelle Obama

'SWEET ENUFF Movement'

CHAPTER 11
Happiness is Fulfilling a Goal

I SAT DOWN IN the driver's seat of my father's white Mercury sedan, closed the door, pulled on my seat belt and, with a racing heartbeat, turned the key.

The day I got my driver's license was the first day of the rest of my life. Years before, I had discovered my love of dance. Now I had found another love. I loved getting behind the wheel and going anywhere and everywhere.

As early as I could remember, I dreamed of moving away. Living with my diabetes stigma and a mentally ill mother kept me focused on getting out of the house. My driver's license brought with it the first real glimmer of hope that liberty was close at hand.

On this particular day I drove myself to dance class. As I walked into the studio, I loudly and conspicuously tossed the keys in my bag. I wanted everyone to know how grown up and independent I was.

After class I got back in the car and drove. I drove way past home. I drove and drove with the radio blasting (even though I was told to keep it off). The day had finally come when I was not reliant on anyone. I was FREE.

I could drive myself to school. I could stop at the store for some Diet Coke. I could leave campus at lunchtime. I didn't have to have my mom or dad tag along when I went to dance class. The feeling of being in control of my life was a new high—and I wanted to chase it indefinitely.

Off to La La Land

Three days after my senior dance performances, in the final days of summer after high school graduation, I landed in New York City. I triumphantly threw myself into school and dance class. Unfortunately, I also began the cycle of extreme binging and purging that would eventually rob me of my sight.

The city was amazing, terrifying, and exciting. I quickly figured out how to get around by mass transit, but I missed driving. Whenever I went home to visit, I couldn't wait to get in the car and go. A year into school and life in New York, I decided to visit Los Angeles to check out the dance scene. As I got into my rented Nissan Sentra at the airport, that sense of freedom immediately returned.

The first time I drove over the 405 pass into the Valley, I was awestruck. *This is it,* I thought. *I need to live here.* I admit it—I was a bit impulsive in my younger days.

I returned to New York City to finish the semester, and by January 1989, I had my own apartment in Van Nuys, California. Up to that point, my tuition and housing had been lumped together as part of my school expenses. My dad had been paying for everything else. For some reason, it had not occurred to me I would have to start paying for my own rent and utilities.

Thanks to the vast expanses of Los Angeles, I also needed a car. Dad and I went to a dealership in Culver City, California, and he bought me a used blue Datsun. It was a stick shift, and I learned to drive a five-speed in the Hollywood Hills.

That feeling had returned. I could go ANYWHERE. And so I drove. I drove over the 405. I drove east into Los Feliz. I drove to the dance studio in North Hollywood. I drove to Laguna Beach. I drove to Disneyland by myself. But I wasn't really by myself. I had my keys.

Detached from Reality

My visual complications began about a year into my new LA life. My sight was not overly affected at first, and it never dawned on me that this great love of mine could ever be in jeopardy. I started at my new school and got a part-time job at the card store. I drove myself to dance class and everywhere else. I also traded in the blue Datsun for my love car, my own blue Nissan Sentra.

As I started to have more procedures, I had a few close calls driving myself home from laser eye surgery. I didn't take the hint. Instead, I tried to outsmart the situation. I would walk over to the movie theater near the hospital and watch a movie while the anesthetic wore off and the pain became tolerable. At the time, I felt so proud of myself for figuring out such a clever solution.

One Sunday afternoon I got in my car to drive a few blocks to Ralph's Grocery Store. As I drove along, my left eye became fuzzy, and a few seconds later, the fuzziness turned to darkness. I made it back to my apartment without injuring myself or anyone else, but that day marked the beginning of the end.

As my visual situation became increasingly worse, I realized I would have to start asking for help. For someone who needed to feel fiercely independent, you might as well have told me life was over.

Over the coming weeks I had a major procedure on my left eye to address the diabetic retinopathy. *How bad can it be?* I thought. *I'm sure he does this kind of procedure every day.*

Everything will be back to normal soon.

Weeks and then months passed after that procedure and my vision had not returned. The worst-case scenario had become reality. My left eye was completely blind.

I was told that many people drive with one functional eye. Then I had a retinal detachment in the right eye. *Am I going to be completely blind?* I suddenly felt crippled. I was having trouble reading and negotiating public spaces. I felt silly and ashamed. I was not willing to give up my passion, so I still attempted to drive in my neighborhood.

On December 7, 1992, I found myself back at the Jules Stein Eye Institute at UCLA to reattach the retina in my right eye. Since my left eye was already blind, the stakes on this procedure were unimaginably high.

I was totally blind following surgery. I also had to stay face down to the floor for weeks to ensure the reattached retina would stay put. It's hard to imagine how tortuous that is unless you've experienced it. I could not lift my head up—not while sleeping or eating or any time in between. My neck and back were in excruciating pain from the contorted positions I was forced to maintain.

My right eye was completely covered so I was totally blind during the entire postoperative recovery period. I barely left my apartment. I feared the worst. I wanted to die.

Death of a Dream

Finally it was time to remove the patch and hold my head upright again. The first thing I remember seeing was the label on a can of apple juice I had been given to treat my low blood sugar.

The surgery worked! I am not totally blind.

More of my vision became restored in my right eye. I did not, however, have any peripheral vision.

I still held on to the hope that I would be able to resume my beloved driving again. Some time after the surgery I got back behind the wheel of my Sentra. It was much scarier now. My depth perception and peripheral vision had become seriously impaired. My reaction time slowed, and I was extremely sensitive to light.

Friends encouraged me to give up the keys. I couldn't imagine life without the ability to move about freely, so I kept going long past all reason and recommendations. I became a menace to the road. It is such a miracle that no one was hurt by my inability to accept my situation.

At just twenty-two years old, my driving days came to an end. First, I had lost my dream of having a professional dance career. Now, I had to give up the car keys, meaning I would never again be able to engage in either of my most profound joys in life.

What could life possibly have in store for me next?

I took a few months to recuperate at my father's home in Florida. However, with no car, I felt more trapped than ever. I returned to LA and decided it was time to do what I was supposed to do. I enrolled in Antioch University in Santa Monica and went to work finishing my bachelor's degree.

I used what few taxi vouchers I was allotted every month for being legally blind and quickly learned how to navigate the local bus system in Santa Monica for most of my transportation needs. I also went into counseling and found support from the Los Angeles Center for the Partially Sighted.

It was uncomfortable, unpleasant, inconvenient, and humbling, but I just kept moving. I was living Step Three of the Victory Dance: Never Give Up.

Life after the Keys

The day I realized I would never again sit in the driver's seat of my blue Sentra was many things: Devastating. Depressing.

Gut wrenching. Restricting. It was also the reality that I had been handed. I couldn't change it.

I could stew in self-pity or move on.

I took the first three steps of the Victory Dance and created a new life for myself. I did not necessarily like my circumstances, but I was determined to keep moving. I accepted this new version of my existence and pressed on, resolved to never give up.

I was also determined not to be dependent on others, so I decided to figure out how to go everywhere using public transportation. This was no easy task living in Los Angeles. The distances between neighborhoods are vast. I often had to leave three or four hours ahead of time in order to make appointments outside of my neighborhood in Santa Monica.

I took the bus to school every day. I enrolled in music classes at UCLA and found the bus that dropped me off right across the street from the music building. I was living Step Three of my Victory Dance, but in the meantime I had quit actual dancing.

Thanks to my binge eating, I put on a lot of weight. I decided to join the famous Gold's Gym in Venice, California, and found myself working out next to Kobe Bryant, Gregory Hines, and a slew of other LA-based celebrities.

I often poked my head into the power dance classes at the gym. *I don't do that anymore*, I'd think as I settled in on the stationary bike. As time passed, I simply couldn't resist the urge. One day I got the nerve up and took a hip hop dance class.

I stood in the back in an attempt to hide. Suddenly I found myself moving again. It was amazing. Afterward the teacher stopped me and thanked me for taking her class. I blushed, far too intimidated to say anything. Encouraged by the teacher's recognition, I returned to the same class the following week. I was starting to get my groove back. I felt so happy to be moving again.

One day I was in the gym on the stationary bike and struck up a conversation with a woman next to me named Janet. She admitted that she had been watching me dance in class. "You are a real dancer, aren't you?"

I looked at Janet in shock. "No, I am legally blind. I am not a dancer anymore."

Janet smiled. "I think you are a dancer. It is just part of you."

She told me she ran a dance camp for kids and was always looking for teachers. She also taught classes in a local Venice beach dance studio, where she worked with a wonderful teacher and choreographer with whom she thought I would connect.

"Oh, you would love this teacher," Janet continued. "I can go with you to her class if you would like."

As she walked away I murmured, "I don't dance anymore. I am blind, and that's that."

I kept running into Janet. She suddenly seemed to be everywhere—in the gym, at the grocery store, and at the coffee shop. Her voice had begun taking up a lot of space in my brain and made me question what I thought was a cold, hard fact about my life. I thought I was done with dance.

Perhaps I had not given up but just taken a break.

Just because I Can

Adjusting to life as a visually impaired person had proven difficult, but I never stopped trying to regain semblances of the life I once knew. I developed a "new normal" way of doing life.

That didn't mean that I was happy about having to make such big adjustments, but I had already used the first steps of my Victory Dance and determined to keep moving. I was in school, making new friends, exploring potential career paths, and putting tremendous effort into staying positive and productive.

Then I met Janet. She saw that dance was my essence. She did not notice that I was visually impaired. She did not care about my inability to drive. She even offered me a ride to class.

She saw me as a whole person in a way that I could no longer see or feel about myself.

I finally conceded to her gentle nudging and attended a dance class. I had yet to be in a dance studio since I had been declared legally blind. I was terrified, sad, curious, and nervous as hell—but I went.

It was like a dead part of me suddenly woke up. Everything came back to me almost instantaneously. The class was low pressure, warm, and inviting. I had been part of such a competitive, high-pressure dance world that it was weird to dance for no other reason than just because I could.

When I mentioned I could not see, the teacher simply said, "OK, we will work it out."

My feelings of fear and shame immediately disappeared.

It had taken some time and coercing, but as it turned out, I never gave up on the most important part of myself. It was still there, waiting to be rediscovered. As I struggled to adapt to life without the luxury of driving, I found a way to connect to myself and start to feel whole again.

While giving up the keys and having to drive my life in a new way was terrifying, I was implementing my own steps to make it work. More significant than any other factor in the process was my decision to never give up.

I kept searching for new ways to live my life. I found new modes of transportation. I figured it out. I never gave up, and because of that decision I found my way back to myself through my first love—dance.

I have not driven a car since 1992. I still miss it, but my life is full and active. I get where I need to go. Life after the keys has become bigger and more expansive than I ever could have imagined when I was face down and blind after retinal surgery.

CHAPTER 12
Having a BIG Dream

AS MUCH AS I'D like to say that everything worked out perfectly from there, those of us who are stubborn know that a dream deferred can be a gut-wrenching experience. I had accepted the fact that I would never drive again. I had also begun to find joy in dance again.

But I was still searching. And I wasn't one to give up. In the midst of my eye surgeries, Michael, my friend and manager from the card store, had introduced me to a surprising source of inspiration.

Michael was absolutely *fixated* on Madonna. At first I did not understand his starstruck infatuation with the pop icon. I grew up in the early 1980s when MTV was actually a music video channel. I saw the original videos for "Borderline," "Lucky Star," and all her other hits from that era. I remember the shots of Madonna rolling around in a white wedding dress next to a lion in her "Like a Virgin" video. I did not much pay attention to her music.

But then I saw her 1990 documentary, *Truth or Dare*.

I had an instant mystic connection to the film. I also knew

many of the dancers featured on the tour. Since I had been forced into early retirement of my own performance career I often lived vicariously through the dance lives of others.

I didn't pay much attention to Madonna's shocking, outlandish shenanigans that were expected from such a film. What struck me were the behind-the-scenes moments and the intensity of producing such a monstrous performance tour.

I was also fascinated by the fact that Madonna had seemed to master the idea that people believe she is important because **she makes them believe** she is important. What I did not know at the time is that this term is called "marketing." And in her case, it was brilliant self-marketing.

I watched the movie so many times I could recite it. How did she pull off such a big event? As a producer in training, I wanted to know how she made it all work and made so much money. My fixation soon led my life down an interesting side street.

Searching for My Lucky Star

When *Truth or Dare* first released I was still in the throes of my eye surgeries and subsequent adjustment to becoming legally blind and giving up my keys. I was also unknowingly obsessed with working even harder to make up for destroying my own life.

Many friends had told me I should become a therapist so I could help others who faced similar adversities to mine. I had another idea—which is why I chose Antioch University. They had a work-study program where you could take courses in an outside institution and get credit toward your degree. *This is perfect*, I thought. I could keep up my crazy artistic adventures by taking outside classes while simultaneously working toward the degree everyone said I had to have to be a "whole and successful person."

The entire 1990s music scene was crawling with stars who

had created fame out of nothing. I decided that if these people could manifest such big things for themselves, then so could I. As part of my school studies, I added a music course from UCLA's extension program. I started piano and voice lessons. I started researching music recording.

I was going to be a rock star! I was as good a dancer as any of the pop icons, and I knew from the grapevine that vocals could be fixed in the studio. How hard could this be, right?

Delusion is a State of Mind

True to form, one part of me was firing on all cylinders. The other part of me knew I was falling deeper and deeper into disassociation and busying myself with pursuing a dead end.

I was a good thirty pounds overweight and did not physically resemble any of the demands of the day for the employment category known as Rock Star. This cold, hard fact did not slow my momentum or intensity.

I searched industry papers and placed a newspaper ad looking for a producer. I wish I had saved it for a good laugh. In the wording, I was specific about wanting to create dance music in the genre of Madonna and Janet Jackson and produced with big dance tours in mind.

Miracle of miracles, the ad was successful! I got a call from a sweet and talented producer named Josch. We met and got along well. I told him I would write the lyrics and he could do the music.

I lived in a studio apartment in Venice, California, about a block from the Venice Boardwalk. Every day, I would take my Walkman with my Madonna tapes and run in the sand, singing as I went. I needed stamina to be a world-class performer, so I ran stairs belting out "Like a Prayer" and "Papa Don't Preach."

Karaoke had also become wildly popular during this time. To improve my vocal skills, I began frequenting local karaoke

Days in LA

bars. I added whatever choreography I could fit onto the tiny stage. In my mind, it was Madison Square Garden.

Here's the thing—no one had the heart to tell me I couldn't really sing. Fortunately for me, Josch was a super talented producer. The tracks were well produced, and they made me sound as strong as possible. Reverb was a highly useful tool in my case.

Once I had everything recorded, I hit the karaoke trail with my CDs. There was a particular gay bar that I liked in West Hollywood called Rage. Monday nights were karaoke night, and I soon became a regular. Kenny, the DJ, was a singer himself, and he let me sing my own stuff. I think he took pity on this chubby, visually impaired white girl who clearly did not belong in a gay club in West Hollywood.

Whenever I would randomly meet some actual music industry insiders, I pursued them like a piranha. I knew I did not fit the look, and I knew I did not have the voice, but I did not care. Madonna pushed her way into the business by pumping her music to club disc jockeys—and learning about her early struggles kept my fantasy in full swing. The disconnection between what was real and what was in my mind was ever growing.

Getting around LA by bus was beginning to take its toll, but I stuck with it and continued my studies. I finally graduated—which meant I was now in possession of a diploma that cost me money I didn't have and made me qualified to do things I had no interest in pursuing.

Even a few years out of eating disorder rehab, my weight still fluctuated like a yo-yo. That was a problem since I decided I needed to have a body like Madonna. And of course, I had my constant companion: diabetes. Between daydream scenarios of touring the world, the rational part of my brain feared my poor health and sight issues would ultimately keep me from achieving *Rolling Stone* cover status.

Nevertheless, I pressed on. I kept up with Patty, my vocal

coach, and my music classes. I eventually started working with another vocal coach, Stephen, whose studio was a good ninety-minute bus ride from where I lived.

Did it make sense to have two vocal teachers? Not really. But I quickly learned that if you offered it, people would *gladly* take your money.

To make matters worse, no one had been willing or able to say to me, "Amy, you can't sing. Stop this now." I'm not sure it would have deterred me anyway. I had learned from *Truth or Dare* that if you make it important enough, people would care.

That's really what I wanted—for people to care. I just wanted somebody to tell me I was OK. A million people at my rock concert would do the trick.

Thank God for Dress Rehearsals

Things started shifting. My friend Patty was moving to Boston with her husband. Going to Rage every week was wearing me down. I hadn't lost any weight. I kept pushing though. I sent my CD and press kit to anyone who would listen. I tried event planners, schools—anybody who I thought might let me sing on a stage somewhere.

By now I had started keeping my musical endeavors to myself, but I did manage to talk myself up to performing a song at a big event in Santa Monica.

When the meeting planners agreed to let me perform, it was based on their knowledge of my dance abilities. I had been dancing frequently with local Santa Monica studios and in local performances.. They knew I was a great dancer, so they believed my self-inflated hype about my music.

In an instant, my rock star hopes were refueled! I had visions of standing next to Madonna, rocking the stage at LIVE AID. I went into action, inviting dance students from a school where I was teaching to be my backup dancers. We rehearsed my Madonna-esque act. They all kept their mouths shut in an act of kindness.

Rehearsal day came and I took the stage with my dancers. Needless to say, my act did not go over well. It was so bad that the meeting planners pulled my act on the spot. Afterward, a friend drove me home who FINALLY and sweetly encouraged me to look more into dancing and less into singing. I was humiliated and relieved at the same time. I was finally free from the shackles of my latest escape plan.

In SGI Nichiren Buddhism we often refer to *protective forces*—not protective in a stereotypical sense, but rather protective in allowing us to be exposed to experiences that allow us to grow or make a change. The closing of my rock star chapter gave me a fresh start to reexamine what I really wanted for my life. I needed a new path. Little did I know that path was three thousand miles away, back home in New York City.

My dreams of rock stardom never came to fruition, but learned that I had the courage to go for the big things—and the courage to walk away.

Let's Do This Thing!

Twelve years of LA life had worn me out, and New York City was calling my name. In 2002, moving across the country without a job or financial backing wasn't exactly the best plan, but I needed a fresh start.

I agreed to take on an apartment in the East Village. The owner was a friend from the gym in LA who rented it to me for a very reasonable amount. I made it seem like I could handle the expense; then came the day of reckoning. She needed the deposit and first month's rent. This is nothing unusual for normal, responsible adults.

I didn't have it.

My friend went ballistic. Looking back, this was one of those moments in which I was forced to take responsibility for my life. I was humiliated and ashamed, and crying got me no sympathy.

"You will come up with the money!" she shouted. "I have bent over backward to make these arrangements for you."

What I did not understand was she had that apartment her entire adult life. It was rent stabilized, and when she worked in Los Angeles, she rented the space to cover the cost. She wasn't even trying to make money off the deal. She was just doing me a solid.

I was backed in a corner. I called my mom, with whom I had no relationship. I also called my dad, who was now broke and nearly homeless. I literally begged and borrowed to get the money together.

As I had been so many other times, I was in way over my head. I didn't even have money for the plane ticket. The mother of a friend gave me a ticket she had gotten through her miles. I boarded the plane with two cartons of belongings, 200 dollars in cash, my father's overused American Express card, and a thin, worn hoodie.

Was I prepared for New York City or what?

I had arranged to stay in a cheap hotel in Midtown Manhattan upon arrival. I handed the desk attendant my father's American Express. The card was declined. I panicked. I called my dad and somehow he made it work—just as he had always done.

My dad is a good man and a kind father, and for some unknown reason, he felt responsible for my diabetes diagnosis as a child and had tried to overcompensate ever since. He just wanted my life to be perfect. After I lost my sight, he swooped in again and tried to make it all better by paying for almost every single expense I had, even if it bankrupted him.

There was a huge part of me that felt desperate to be on my own. I wanted to earn my own money and be independent. The bigger part of me was conditioned to the idea that I was "sick" and would always need someone to take care of me.

My second day back in NYC I went to my new apartment on E. 7th Street in the famous East Village. *This is where Madonna got her start!* I thought to myself. What I failed to realize (and never thought to inquire about) was that the apartment was a fifth-floor walk up. Not so great for someone who is legally blind.

It was an immaculate space, and my friend made it clear she wanted it kept that way. By now, I was terrified of her. I was terrified of New York. I feared I would not be able to survive. I kept smiling and chanting. Hey, at least now I could get around easily without a car.

Dumb and Dumber

Life in New York City can be harsh, especially when you are naïve and broke. I managed to get the rent paid every month, mostly through credit card manipulation. My father was no longer in a position to help with any consistency, and at thirty-two years old, it was time I figured out how to take care of my own life.

I found some odd jobs, and for the first time in my life, I was forced to really work. After six months I had convinced myself I could pay twice as much rent and agreed to move into the apartment of a friend who was leaving for the winter. I was soon spending basically my entire paycheck on rent.

I existed in a constant state of panic. On some days, I didn't even have money for food. To keep a roof over my head, I moved every nine months for the first three years I was back in New York.

Desperate for something good to come out of my existence, I decided to revive my SWEET ENUFF Movement. While much of my work with the kids was sincere, I was also secretly hoping to get press for myself. Life was getting too hard, and I was blending in too well as just another nameless, faceless worker bee. I needed everyone to be in awe of my ever-continuous plight to overcome adversity.

It was a strange time. I was like a wounded bird battling to catch its wind and fly ahead. I had no sense of myself, no interest in taking responsibility for my life, and I existed by reacting to whatever situation appeared next in front of me.

I hid my true feelings and was afraid all the time. Longing for a relationship yet too afraid to communicate, I just made myself, and probably a lot of other people around me, crazy. This is also when I met Tom, the man who would become a huge focus of my mental and emotional energy.

Every day felt like I was trudging through molasses. Still, I seemed to always keep moving. I kept chanting and stayed connected to my friends in faith in the SGI. This was my lifeline.

I was gathering a valuable skill set without even knowing it. Somehow, through poverty, near homelessness, and the demise of my rock star fantasy, I never gave up. Maybe it was pure panic that kept me going, or perhaps somewhere deep inside, I knew things would work out.

My fantasy life had become a huge wellspring of hope, and it worked for the time. I was able to get up in the morning, chant, and make causes to address my immediate needs for my life. Eventually I landed in a relatively stable living situation and started earning some real money. This brief stability would ground me for what was yet to come.

What keeps pushing you forward? Is it grounded in reality, or are you chasing your own rock star fantasy? I would never tell anyone to give up on a dream—I just want you to be honest with yourself for a moment and examine your motives.

Are your dreams and goals for the greater good? Are you working toward building something better for others? If so, I believe there is no force strong enough to stop you!

CHAPTER 13
You're Gonna Be Rich!

IT STARTED LITERALLY MOMENTS after I got to the emergency room.

"Are you going to sue?"

"You are going to be so rich."

It came from people I knew and from people just standing around who heard I had been run over by a New York City Transit bus.

I didn't even know if my right leg was still attached to my body, and they wanted to know whether a team of lawyers was en route, armed, and ready to wreak financial havoc on the bad guys.

In the emergency room the night of the accident, a representative from the New York City Transit stopped in to visit. I was flat on my back on a gurney behind a curtain in the ER.

He seemed like a nice enough guy. He asked me a few questions, but I can't remember what they were. I do remember smiling at him (I often just smiled at everyone by default) and saying something like, "Oh, it's not that bad. I'm sure I'll be home in a few days."

Fortunately I did not sign anything to that effect before he left.

That first week it became apparent that my situation was beyond critical. I was given constant high doses of painkillers, making me dazed and disoriented around the clock.

Friends and fellow Buddhists were coming to visit in droves. A few days after the accident a friend stopped in to visit who was very insistent that I hire an attorney immediately.

"Oh, it's not that bad," I said. "I'm sure I'll be home in a few days."

My friend kept coming to see me and insisted that I see an attorney. She was rather dramatic about her request, and it was starting to annoy me. I am not a sue-happy person, and I didn't want to bother. I was too busy trying to stay alive.

Thanks to my friend's determination, I finally agreed to talk to some legal counsel. Three attorneys were recommended, and each came to visit me. It was not even one week after my accident. My leg was crushed and had no skin. I was high on painkillers and full of tubes.

The first attorney was a young man in a brown suit. I don't recall his name, so we'll call him Mr. Brown Suit. He sat down on the edge of my bed and seemed a bit overwhelmed by the sight of this woman lying there with her leg held together by huge metal rods. I'll admit it was an intimidating view—the external fixator looked like a massive erector set that was literally holding all the broken pieces of me in place.

He smiled nervously, took a breath, and tried to impress me with his credits, education, and legal acumen. Mr. Brown Suit concluded his monologue with, "I will get you millions of dollars."

I swear I could see actual dollar signs in his eyes. The room grew silent. I stared at him sitting there in his little brown suit and wondered where he was going after he left my hospital room. Would he have a drink, go to the gym, or meet up with his girlfriend? What nice, normal thing was he planning to do while I lay there looking like Humpty Dumpty?

I thanked him for his time. "I have a few other attorneys to meet." I also reminded him I was not certain I would be alive from day to day and that I was seeking an advocate, not a paycheck.

Subtle, right? I was far too polite to say what I was really thinking.

The amount of money this accident was going to cost had not yet begun to dawn on me. All I was concerned with at this point was staying alive and keeping my leg attached to my body.

Mr. Brown Suit left, and I think I literally threw up.

The next day, lawyer number two came by to visit. He was a strapping young guy named Steve who had been referred by a colleague.

Steve was way too excited for my senses. The dollar signs in his eyes outshone the dollar signs in Mr. Brown Suit's eyes. Steve went on at length about how he had a friend in the legal department at the New York City Transit.

Okay, I kept thinking. *So what?*

"I can get you ten million dollars," Steve finally blurted out.

Again, I had no response. I wondered whether Steve had a hot date waiting or if he was planning to hook up with someone at his favorite yuppie bar after he left me fighting for my life.

I am the type of person who does not react to things immediately. I prefer to think before I respond. I thanked Steve for stopping by and reminded him I needed to get some sleep as I was scheduled for surgery the following morning.

"Oh", he responded, his face steeped in disappointment. I guess he thought that his promise of a ten-million-dollar payout should have had me signing on the dotted line right then and there.

Steve left and I asked for more painkillers. I just wanted to check out.

The next day came and brought with it Andy. I liked Andy from the moment he arrived. He shook my hand and asked how I was feeling. He remarked how sorry he was that I had suffered this terrible accident. He sat down and with a warm tone we began to chat. He had represented a client who was a friend of a friend. He had won her case.

Andy was straight with me.

"Look Amy, this is the New York City Transit you are dealing with. They are horrible. I will tell you up front that the case will be long, and it will be ugly. They will lie, they will cheat, they will deal, they will make your life a living hell, and they will blame you or anyone else they can. What I can also tell you is that we have gone up against New York City Transit before, and while I can't promise you anything, I can promise we will do our best to get this done for you."

Andy then sat back in his chair, shrugged his shoulders, and smiled.

"I like you," I said.

The next day Andy became my attorney, my advocate, and my friend.

Just Put It On My Tab

As was the case so many other aspects of my life after the accident, I had NO idea how bad things would get. In this case, I'm talking about my money situation. There was simply no way I or anyone else could have never predicted how destitute I would eventually become.

Andy had gone right to work handling the legal details of my case and bringing suit against New York City Transit. He gave me his personal cell phone number and told me to call any time and for any reason. He was always pleasant and took my calls, and he never left me wondering what was happening with my case.

When I was transferred from the local hospital to the burn ICU at New York Presbyterian Hospital, it was Andy who was standing there when I opened my eyes the first morning. My sister had not yet arrived from Maryland, so Andy wanted to make sure I had a smooth transfer and wouldn't have to worry about all the paperwork. He handled everything.

I remember waving to Andy that first morning and thanking him before falling back into a drug-induced sleep.

For some reason (we'll blame it on the drugs) it never occurred to me that life would keep going during my extended hospital stay. The bills did not stop. The rent had to be paid. While I had a small savings, I certainly did not have a backup plan that was able to manage the size and scope of the situation I now had on my hands.

When I was ready to be discharged from months in intensive care, Andy made sure I had money to cover my living expenses. He didn't pull any punches about how much money this would cost me. He told me that the companies who loan to patients in situations like mine were not regulated. I would have to pay as much as 29 percent interest on the money I was borrowing against my lawsuit.

I did not have many other options—and the loan company was well aware of this fact. I certainly was in no shape to go back to work. I could barely stand on my own two feet.

All I knew was that with a loan, I had some money in the bank. In my mind I would be back to work in no time. How could I have possibly foreseen that I would spend the next five years either having or recovering from surgery and infection?

My new state of existence outside the hospital was extremely expensive. I needed care at home that insurance often did not cover. I was too weak for public transportation, and car and taxi services were eating away at my exceptionally insufficient nest egg.

In December 2009, four months after I got home from my initial nursing home stay, I was in surgery yet again. The constant surgery continued into spring 2010. The severe bacterial infection in my bones would simply not cooperate.

In February 2010, in the dead of a brutal winter, I found myself back in the nursing home for a second stay. Even though I still owed them five thousand dollars from the last time I was there, Andy worked his magic so I could get the care and antibiotic treatment I needed to stay alive. We soon found out that I would need another course of six-week intravenous antibiotics to battle my unyielding infection.

Another six weeks in this nursing home? I couldn't even stomach the thought of it.

I was informed my insurance would only pay for the drugs if they were administered at the nursing home. If I wanted to have home health care and administer the treatments myself I would have to pay cash up front.

How much could it be? I thought. The representatives from the treatment company came to visit at the hospital and cut right to the chase. "It will cost $7,000 for you to continue the treatment at home. Oh, and we need proof of funds before we can do anything."

"What do you think I am? A bank?" I blurted out in frustration.

"Well, your insurance will cover the full cost of your six-week stay at the nursing home."

For people who are around sick and injured patients all day long, the home care administrators didn't seem to understand that those of us who have been in and out of hospitals and operating rooms are not rolling in bags of cash. I guess they assumed Andy and my attorneys had endless wads of it at their disposal.

It didn't matter to me that insurance would cover the cost at the nursing home. Staying there for another six weeks of my life was not an option. I procured a way to borrow the money outright. There was NO WAY I was spending another six weeks in that nursing home.

So I added another $7,000 to my mounting debt, which was staggering. The first hospital bill I received was for $138,948.72. That was for the treatment on May 1, 2009. Just that one day.

The envelopes were coming almost daily. I didn't even bother to look after a while. Once a week I put them in an envelope and sent them directly to Andy. I did not want to know.

In 2010 I applied for New York State Medicaid and was temporarily granted support. When my renewal came due, I was informed that because I had been paying taxes prior to my accident, I was receiving an "unusually high" amount of disability income. As a result, in order for me to continue to receive Medicaid, I would have to pay an $879 per month spend down.

The "unusually high" amount of disability I had been receiving did not even cover my rent and food. I ended up applying for emergency food stamps so I could eat. In order to be granted emergency food stamps, a person has to prove they have less than $100 total monies. This was no problem for me.

The loan shark company had decided it was too risky to continue to assist my situation. Despite the overwhelming evidence that they were most likely going to be repaid plus 29 percent interest, they cared not.

Finally in September 2010, the sharks gave me one final loan for $3,500. At the time it seemed like millions of dollars.

I kept thinking I would get back to work. While I was not physically (or emotionally) able to handle any of my former jobs, I kept searching. I was so ready to start to see some type of normal life return.

There were lots of times when I wanted to give up. Sometimes late at night, I'd wonder why I was still here. Why couldn't some-one just put me out of my misery?

Pity parties may feel cathartic in the moment, but they are also dangerous. Self-pity and despair are the kinds of mindsets that take hold in our brains and never let go. I didn't let those thoughts fester. I couldn't.

Despite the reality in front of me, I continued to chant and to hold on to the belief that these days were merely the storm before the calm.

I certainly felt like I had been through a whole lot more storms than my fair share, but feeling sorry for myself wasn't going to change that. So I vowed to never give up, and to keep looking ahead, not down or behind me.

CHAPTER 14
Tell the Truth, Please

CURIOSITY OFTEN CAUSES PEOPLE to forget some basic principles about respect, privacy, and common courtesy. It seemed every day someone else was asking me about my lawsuit. Strangers and friends alike loved to ask me how much money I thought I'd get.

Was it any of their business? I felt like snapping back with my own inappropriate, rude questions like, "Did you ever get that rash looked at?" "Why don't you finally start that diet?" Or maybe, "How's that bitter divorce coming along?" Instead I opted for the high road most of the time and attempted to change the subject to literally anything else.

In October 2010, as if I did not have enough to manage, I started feeling funny. I noticed I became short of breath just walking down the street. I visited one of my doctors and asked him to indulge me and do an EKG. Sure enough the cardiac test came back irregular, and I was immediately sent downstairs to the cardiologist.

Dr. Yaghoobzadeh, otherwise known as Dr. Y, was soft spoken and calm as he chatted with me about my symptoms and my situation. He suggested a stress test and encouraged me to get it done right away. *Great,* I thought. *Now what?*

Sure enough, I failed the test, and the next day I was scheduled for an angioplasty to have a stent put in my heart.

"Heart surgery?" I sobbed to Dr. Y. "What's wrong with me now? This is like my fifteenth surgery in seventeen months!"

The cable in my apartment had been disconnected due to lack of payment. I called my dad and asked if he could pay the bill. If I had to have heart surgery, at least I wanted to be able to watch TV.

On October 1, 2010, I went in for the angioplasty. The procedure was a success. If you are at risk for heart disease I HIGHLY recommend doing whatever you can to prevent any kind of heart surgery.

It is not fun.

Dr. Y walked up to me after the procedure as I lay on the gurney in the operating room.

"The procedure is a success," he said. "You don't need open heart surgery."

Open heart surgery, what the fuck? Does this nightmare ever end? Even the reference to it made me numb.

I have been under Dr. Y's care since that day and am happy to report that with a clean diet, daily exercise, intense blood glucose monitoring, and managed medication my cardiac condition is completely stable.

In the midst of everything else, in fall 2011, I lost my apartment. In 2006 I had moved in with a friend in her rent-stabilized apartment. We knew the building was after the unit, and not long after I moved in, they saw their chance. My friend suffered a stroke while visiting family over the holidays and was unable to return home to New York City. The building got wind of what was going on, and thus ensued a horrible court battle—and I was very much caught in the middle.

Andy again came to the rescue and got me a kick-ass lawyer who agreed to represent me in housing court in exchange for a lien on my case to cover her fees. *HOUSING COURT? Are you f'ing kidding me?* I certainly did not have cash to pay legal fees. The lawyer did an amazing job of delaying the case as long as she could, allowing me to keep a roof over my head.

By early November 2011, the building had had enough back and forth. They sent a social service worker to see me. She reported that I was not disabled, despite the fact I was still on a walker and unable to leave the apartment on some days for food. In fact, the first day she came to see me was just a few weeks post op from my heart surgery.

To this day I believe she must have been paid by the building to file the report against me, but we will never know for sure. I was evicted in December 2011. With no cash, no credit, and very little energy, I now had to move. I kept chanting through all the insanity.

I found myself back on Craigslist looking for a roommate situation like a twenty-something kid who had just moved to New York City. Broke, broken, and now homeless, I thought it really couldn't get much worse.

The attorney helping me with housing court had become my friend. She swooped in and saved the day. Her neighbor was leaving New York and was willing to let me rent her apartment at significantly less rent than market value. Miraculously, the building had an elevator and laundry room! These were never things I needed in the past, but since I was no longer able to climb stairs, any type of walk-up apartment was not an option.

I moved into the warm and cozy space on W. 108 Street. Two weeks after the move I had yet another surgery to remove the external fixator that had been implanted in September 2011. It was a quick outpatient procedure. However, I was yet again not able to put full weight on my right leg. I found myself back on a walker, struggling to move.

The final loan money had run out, and I was scraping by on disability and food stamps. It was December, and the weather was bad. I locked myself up in my apartment. *I can't do this anymore*, I thought. I stopped answering the phone, watched a lot of TV, and stayed in bed or on the couch around the clock, mostly because I was too afraid to go anywhere.

Blame it on the weather, but that was an especially dark and lonely time in my life. I know I had been in worse situations before, but I couldn't help feeling like this was the low point in a life heavily punctuated by other low points.

Darkness Before the Dawn

As Andy had predicted, our fight with the New York City Transit legal team turned ugly. They actually had the nerve to have the bus driver who ran over me testify that I walked into the bus while it was not moving. Yes, that's correct—not moving.

At the time of the accident there had serendipitously been an ambulance parked about a half a block away from the scene. New York City Transit sunk even lower when they filed suit against the ambulance company for blocking the crosswalk, even though they were almost a full block away at the time of impact.

In truth, if that ambulance had not been so close, I probably would have bled to death waiting for EMS to arrive on a busy Friday afternoon in New York City.

The lawsuit against the ambulance company was eventually dismissed but delayed the case a good year or more. In fact, they delayed every deposition and court date they could. Andy and the legal team did their best to stay positive, but that was not an easy task.

In the meantime, I had become reliant on the generosity of friends for things like food and toiletries. I managed somehow to make rent every month but there was nothing left over. I was afraid to leave the house, fearing that if something happened I would not have money to get home or protect myself.

I made a brief attempt to get back to work as a fitness trainer. The hours standing in the gym wreaked havoc on my leg and the pain became unbearable. I quit after two weeks.

In summer 2013 my marathon pseudorelationship with Tom finally collapsed, as he was, by then, in a serious long-term relationship with someone else. I went completely manic. While I knew the situation was crazy, something about it was comfortably familiar. Finding out (via Facebook) his new girlfriend had moved in for good sent me over the edge.

I emailed Andy in a very Jerry Maguire moment of desperation and expressed my extreme discontent at the unfairness of it all and my grievance with the universe.

I had always tried to be a "good girl." I was nice (maybe too nice) to everyone I encountered. I had spent my whole life hiding my pain. Now I began questioning everything about my past and present. Nothing about the way I had been doing my life was working. It was all broken. If it hadn't been for consistently chanting Nam Myoho Renge Kyo, I am not sure I would have survived.

I became so destitute that my psychologist finally referred me to an outreach organization for people with no resources. Humiliated and alone, I met with them and they agreed to cover one month of utility expenses. *It's something*, I thought.

In the snow-packed winter of 2013, the owner of my apartment let me know that in the spring she would be listing the apartment to sell. I knew going into the situation she would eventually want to sell, but why now? The weather was unbearable, and I didn't even have enough money for food.

I swallowed hard. By this point I had become completely disassociated from the world and from myself. I had not been able to recreate anything that even remotely resembled my life from before, and I was tired of trying.

The apartment sold relatively quickly, and I was informed I would need to move out by February 1, 2014, smack dab in the middle of the coldest, snowiest part of the season. I had to laugh. How on earth did I go from working, dancing, and living my life to being crippled, homeless, and on food stamps?

As an SGI Nichiren Buddhist, I knew I was supposed to never give up and always have hope, but honestly, I wasn't feeling it at all. The shame about my life in general was too much to bear.

You have probably heard the idea that "life never gives you more than you can handle." I always thought that was a crock of bull. It was just one of those clichés that people say that makes them sound wise or something.

I'm here to tell you that by November 2013, it felt like life had handed me a big, steaming pile of crap, and that pile had reached maximum capacity. I was out of ideas, out of time, out of options, out of money, out of energy, and out of patience.

I definitely felt like life had given me more than I could handle.

I kept doing what I had to do, though. What other option did I really have? I humbly accepted money and dinner gifts from friends. I kept up a good front. Tom had recently gotten married, so the dream of that relationship ever rekindling was gone forever.

Andy stood by me the entire time. He promised me they would get it done. He frequently reminded me what New York City Transit was doing was exactly what he had told me the day we met in that hospital room in 2009. He told me to try and not worry.

Easier said than done.

CHAPTER 15
Impacting Others

I TRIED MY BEST to take all the well-meaning advice to heart—and believe me when I say that I got A LOT of advice.

I tried to "not worry." I tried to "hold on to hope." I tried to believe that everything would "work out for the best." Those all feel pretty meaningless when you are busy figuring out how you will eat your next meal.

But I kept chanting. I chanted for justice. A friend had encouraged me to chant for the truth to be revealed, for the judge to see the lawsuit for what it was, and especially for the humanity and happiness of the representatives of New York City Transit to emerge.

She encouraged me to chant that they find it in their hearts to do the right thing. While this idea made me furious, I knew she was right. I was being tested beyond the maximum capacity I thought I could manage, but I kept chanting with her guidance in mind.

Andy and my legal team assured me that we would definitely be going to trial. I, on the other hand, was hoping for a settlement. Not only would a trial be long and ugly, but I also felt it would lead to a long appeal process after the verdict and delay my future even more.

We were finally granted a hearing with the judge in early December 2013. She apologized for the amount of time it took to get the meeting. The delay tactics that the New York City Transit had employed had been highly effective. The judge denied their attorney any of the motions he requested in their attempt to delay even more. She also assigned us a trial date in mid-February 2014.

Finally, we had a date. I was sitting in the back of the courtroom the day of the hearing wearing a long black dress. When the New York City Transit lawyer came to the back of the room, I lifted up the bottom of my dress enough to expose my crushed, deformed leg. I saw him catch a glimpse as he quickly moved to sit on the bench behind me, where my leg would no longer be visible.

Yes, I thought. *There is an ACTUAL person here you are toying with. What will you tell your kids tonight about what you do for a living?*

With a trial date on the calendar, Andy and the legal team were excited. Having that date gave me hope that we were nearing a resolution, and I would finally be allowed to start planning the rest of my life.

Physically I was improving. I had been surgery free since February 2012. My surgical team had finally found the root of my bacterial infection. My cardiac situation was stable. I was somewhat less afraid when I went to sleep at night that I would not wake up in the morning. I was being medicated for my PTSD so I could at least function on a basic level.

Since being given the notice to vacate, I found a room in the apartment of a friend who lived in the same neighborhood. The room wasn't much—and I was going to be sharing it and a bathroom with four other girls. For a forty-four-year-old woman, this was pretty humiliating.

Then Andy called.

"You are never going to believe this," he began. "New York City Transit has agreed to meet us in mediation toward an out-of-court settlement. Don't get too excited, but we have a date. It's February fifth."

How could I not get excited? This legal case had been hanging over me around the clock, clouding my recovery and keeping me from being able to move on and rebuild my life. I had to watch everything I said and did. I became paranoid, wondering if the New York City Transit representatives were following me, trying to prove I was not as seriously injured as I claimed.

But I kept moving. I thought about the guidance my friend had given me, and I truly chanted that the goodness of the people on the other side would emerge.

It Just Had to Snow, Didn't It

Good timing has never seemed to be on my side. In the middle of the nastiest winter I can remember, I had to move out of my cozy apartment on February first and into a shared room. The move also happened to fall on the day before the mediation. I did not sleep a wink that first night in my new space. My entire future rested on what would happen in the next twenty-four hours.

I borrowed a few dollars and took myself out for a good breakfast. After I finished my meal, I planned to take the subway to the building in Times Square where the mediation was scheduled to take place.

On the day of the mediation, there was a massive snow, sleet, and ice storm. The entire city ground to a halt. Roads shut down and the trains stopped running. New York City was basically a ghost town compared to its normal hustle and bustle pace.

I left in plenty of time to arrive at the building early, but I got to the subway to discover it was not running. The weather was so bad it had literally shut down the train at rush hour.

My legal team called and asked if I wanted to reschedule. *You've got to be kidding me.* "NO!" I replied. I wouldn't give up now. I'd find a way.

This proved to be harder than I thought. I was still using a crutch, and I discovered that moving around in the snow on foot was almost impossible. There were no buses or taxis to be seen. I felt the panic rise in my body.

I hobbled one block over to a less busy street. I kept chanting under my breath and fighting not to fall on the sleet and ice. Random people stopped to keep me from falling as I trudged along.

I made it to the corner of the next block in one piece and put my hand out to hail a cab. As I did, a cab immediately pulled up and dropped off a lovely man who held the door for me.

"Congratulations," he said. "It's rough out here today."

"You have no idea," I responded, immensely grateful to him for his assistance.

The taxi driver slowly made his way through the storm and successfully dropped me off one block from my destination. As I opened the taxi door, two construction workers saw my crutch and stopped what they were doing to help me navigate the piles of icy sleet and snow.

They walked me the entire block into the building. I held back tears in my eyes for such a random act of support and kindness.

No surprise—the weather had delayed everyone. I was actually the first person to arrive. I sat in silence as the lawyers and representatives from New York City Transit arrived, followed by Andy and my attorneys, and finally the judge.

They sat me down in a conference room and disappeared. I

could barely breathe. Across the hall sat a group of people very much deciding what direction the rest of my life would go.

I Wish You Good Health

The room where I waited had big glass windows, allowing me to see the snow and sleet that now blanketed New York City. As the hours ticked by, Andy stopped in to check on me from time to time and keep me updated. It was torture.

By early afternoon my attorneys came into the room with definite excitement in their faces. "It's going well," they said—whatever that meant.

At one point during the mediation, the judge came in with one of my lawyers. As he shook my hand, I asked my attorney if I could show the judge my leg. I pulled up my pants leg, and the judge flinched.

Part of me doubted him. At this point, after nearly five years of surgery, debilitating poverty, grief, pain, and mind-numbing isolation, I wasn't trusting of anything, anyone, myself, or the world around me. I was just tired.

I pulled a chair away from the conference table that by now was lined with coffee cups and stared out the window at the gloomy February day. *This has to resolve now*, I thought in my heart. *When this happens today—and it will happen today—I will create value in the world. I don't know how, but I will.*

Once again I determined my victory.

A few moments later Andy and my other two lawyers came bustling into the room. David, my trial attorney, sat down next to me. "They made an offer."

I stared at him blankly as he told me what it was. I was dumbfounded.

"We are not done yet. We just need to know if you are willing to work with this."

"Yes! Please, just wrap this up," I pleaded.

They left the room. I felt numb. The amount was significantly more than I had hoped for. I called a financial planner who had been recommended by a friend. I had no idea how to handle everything flying around me and felt the need to start planning immediately.

Less than an hour later my team came back into the room. David sat down, pulled up a chair, and took a deep breath. "That initial offer is no longer valid."

I was stricken with fear.

"We got even **MORE**."

I had tears of relief, anger, suffering, and loneliness. I wasn't happy. I wasn't sad. I just cried.

Had I kept moving long enough and hard enough to see the light of a new life? Had I actually manifested a settlement that was something I deserved and brought justice to an organization notorious for ripping people off and skirting responsibly? Had I done it?

My mind was racing. A few minutes later Andy came in with the documents. I signed on the dotted line.

I thought about that day in the hospital just days after the accident. I thought about how Andy had predicted how hard, ugly, and long a process this was going to be to the end. I thought about how he said they would get it done. He had been right on all counts.

One of the most surreal moments of the day came on the way out of the building. We all ended up in the elevator together—me, Andy, my two attorneys, and the lawyer and representative from New York City Transit. The representative looked at me squarely in the eyes and said, "Ms. Jordan, I know you have had a difficult time, and I wish you good health."

The moment fell silent.

My prayers had been answered. I had chanted for the humanity of the representatives from New York City Transit to emerge and for them to simply do the right thing.

It was after 4 p.m., and the sleet and snow had stopped by the time we walked out of the building. David handed me $40 for a cab. I still had almost no money in hand, and it would be several more months until funds were released.

I took myself out to dinner that night and sat there at that table for a long time. *What now?* I thought.

The events of the past five years were racing through my head. *Who am I anymore?* I really had no idea. I was tired and still numb. It had all taken so long, but at the same time, it had all happened so fast.

I survived by doing Step Three of my Victory Dance. I never gave up no matter how crazy it got. I kept showing up and making a way. When I couldn't buy groceries, I found food stamps. When I lost one place to live, I found another. When one doctor said we'd have to amputate, I found other doctors willing to try to save my leg.

I fought for my life with everything in me. At times when I was so depressed that I couldn't even manage to get out of bed, I just chanted while staring at the ceiling. Eventually I got myself up and took care of the next task at hand.

Sitting at dinner that night after my case settled I took a deep breath. *I will keep moving,* I promised myself. *And I will make good on that promise. I will create value.*

Life is full of joy, but it's also full of disappointments. That's not me being pessimistic—it's called real life. Real life is really messy.

Yes, I do have to take insulin shots every day. I am not a professional dancer on Broadway. I am legally blind. I can no longer drive. I have a rebuilt leg and some new skin that cost a few million dollars. I went through a five-year lawsuit. I'm not married to the man of my dreams.

But yes, I'm still here. I'm still leaving my mark on the world, making meaningful connections, and working harder than ever to create value.

It's easy to give up. That's why so many people do it! But it's also why we see so much sadness in the world. When you throw in the towel, it doesn't make any of those disappointments go away. They're still there—all you've done is thrown regret into the mix.

Choose to keep fighting. Decide right now that you will take just one step forward today. Just one. That's all it takes to keep going and create your Victory Dance.

I spoke recently with Andy. We stay in regular communication. He mentioned that not long ago he had run into the judge who mediated my case on February 5, 2014. Almost four years to the day later the judge remembered me by name. He remembered the gory specifics of the accident. The judge asked Andy how was I doing now.

Andy reminded me this judge oversees hundreds of cases a year but my circumstances and the miraculous resolution had never left his memory.

My prayer had truly been answered.

Step Four
Courage

CHAPTER 16
I Just Want to Fit In

THE WORD "COURAGE" IS one of those terms I hear frequently thrown around in modern culture. According to its formal definition, courage is, "The quality of mind or spirit that enables a person to face difficulty, danger, pain, etc., without fear."

I don't think the absence of fear represents courage at all. That doesn't even make sense to me. Who doesn't feel fear?

Someone very wise once said that, "Courage is to feel the fear and do it anyway." That description feels much better. I believe true courage is the ability to move forward in your life in spite of the fear. It's being able to say, "I see you, Fear. You can stick around if you want, but I've got things to do."

That's what Step Four in the Victory Dance is all about. When you face difficulty and feel the fear that comes with it, this next step means moving forward regardless of what seemingly crazy circumstances you encounter.

Being fearless and being courageous really are two different things. I am not even sure it's possible to *never* feel fear. President Franklin D. Roosevelt once said, "The only thing we have to fear is fear itself." While that advice sounded great, I wasn't so sure.

Fear reminds me I'm doing something that is propelling my life forward. There have been countless rehearsals where I walked into a room full of some of the most seasoned, in-demand dancers in the business. They are all standing there, just waiting for me to open my mouth and create something amazing through their movement.

And I'm not supposed to feel a little healthy fear?

I try to be prepared, but sometimes the ideas don't work, time runs short, or I can't quite figure out which direction to go.

I show up anyway and—as we have discussed frequently in this book—**simply keep moving forward. I have become more comfortable with allowing myself to be uncertain and to try things out that may not work.** After all, that is what rehearsal is for, right?

Life is the same. Sometimes things work, sometimes they don't, and sometimes we may feel fearful, embarrassed, or un-certain. These are 100 percent valid feelings! In fact, sitting with the discomfort of a situation or series of steps that may not be working is often how I have found the wisdom to make changes, try different things, and finally come to a resolution.

Fear isn't a sign of weakness—it's a gauge for whether or not you are doing something to move ahead and continue your Victory Dance. When you can take that next step in spite of the fear, that's when a beautiful dance manifests.

So before we round into the final step of our Victory Dance, let's talk about what it means to find the courage to keep mov-ing past the fear and doubt that we all encounter.

Oh C'mon, Not on the Costume!

Fear and doubt were two feelings I was familiar with long before I set foot into my first elementary classroom. It was the late 1970s and my family and I were living in an affluent South

Florida suburb. On the surface, we were a nice, normal little family. My dad was a successful ophthalmologist and active member of our community, and my mom was a homemaker. She had a pretty significant mental illness, and as a kid, I never understood why she was always talking to herself.

My diabetes diagnosis at age four had been an obvious blow to the entire family. In those days there were few effective treatments for type 1 diabetes. We did not know about carb counting or blood glucose testing.

What I did know is that for every dance or class I attended, a parent had to be with me. My other constant companion was this wicker box filled with candy and apple juice in case I had a hypoglycemic reaction.

I didn't see any other kids with wicker baskets. I got the memo early on that I was different. I hated it.

By mid-elementary school my rebellion was in full swing. I was sneaking candy and other sweets any chance I could get. This is when the two distinct parts of myself first began to develop. There was Normal Amy who I wanted everyone to see, who didn't need special treatment and who could do anything that any other normal kid could do. Then there was Disorder Amy, the weirdo who felt sick and had a stupid basket with her all the time.

Even at a young age, I really thought I was fooling everyone—that is, until the beginning of every school year. My parents would call a special meeting with all my teachers so they could discuss my condition. I dreaded those meetings and resented my parents for calling them. I got stuck with the "weird" label before I ever had a chance to prove otherwise.

After being called out time and time again, my life's pursuit eventually became to stand out for all the *right* reasons. I wanted to be seen and heard for what I did rather than what I appeared to be on the surface—a sickly kid who would always be different.

I had also been deemed "gifted." This was no great honor in my eyes. My mother was all about having a trophy child, so I did not have much say in the matter. Deep down, I did not really feel as smart as the other kids in my class.

Ms. Guiliano was my fourth-grade gifted and talented teacher. She scared the living daylights out of me. I had this intense urge to slink under my desk every time she walked by. She was tall with dark hair and a big nose. I had an active imagination and wondered what her life was like outside school walls. Maybe she was a witch, and at night, her mustang convertible transformed into a broom.

Ms. Guiliano was set to direct the school play that year, which just so happened to be *Romeo and Juliet*. I wasn't going to let her presence stop me from trying out. Always wanting to be the star, I vied for the top billing, or at the very least, the big solo part in the dance segment. Even in fourth grade, I needed to do the most.

I was denied both the lead part and the solo dance sequence and was instead relegated to "chorus member."

Like every activity in which I participated, there was much ado about my diabetes. My parents were sure to have snacks arranged, and my mom would often come and stay during the entire rehearsal. It was mortifying.

The popular and beautiful kids had all the big parts. As part of Juliet's chorus, I did a lot of dancing and was determined to stand out. I danced bigger and harder than I ever had. Ms. Guiliano would pound on the piano and remind us to keep the focus on Juliet. I think she was talking directly to me.

One rehearsal I was prancing in a circle with the other chorus members. I felt funny and dizzy, and I started screaming and acting out. Ms. Guiliano stopped playing and came to center stage to discipline me for my rude behavior.

Then everything went black. The next thing I remember was

lying on the ground with everyone looking down at me. I felt sick and woozy. All the kids dressed in their Shakespearean costumes were staring at me wide eyed and in shock.

"What's wrong with her?"

"Is she dead?"

"Is she retarded?"

A moment later someone was pouring orange juice into my mouth. I could barely swallow. "Drink this," an adult voice said. "Drink it all."

I started to choke. No one seemed to care that my costume was now covered in sloppy, sticky orange juice. I wished a magic hole would open up and swallow me so I could escape the stares of confusion and disgust.

My dad ran toward the stage as Ms. Guiliano was holding my head up. They picked me up off the floor and guided me into the school office. My mother, with her ever-dependable flare for the dramatic, came running into the office out of breath with panic-stricken eyes. I crouched down in my chair.

The thing I have learned about hypoglycemia is that once the juice, candy, or glucose kicks into my system I have a pretty fast recovery time. It just took a few sips, and I'd start to feel better within a few minutes following an episode.

That didn't matter. The damage was done. This type of situation was exactly what I always feared. I also felt incredibly ashamed of my parents' need to overreact. To their credit, it was the 1980s and diabetes treatment was not nearly as advanced or understood.

And to my credit I shook the entire thing off like a champ. As I had learned to do so well, I showed up at rehearsal the next day and acted like nothing had happened. I was determined to shine through my dancing and outperform even the leads.

I wanted to beat this stigma and just be normal. I dreamed of getting the chance to prove my worth without the labels. It seems I would be destined to chase that dream for much of my life, only to have it deferred.

I Am Not My Condition

As an elementary-age child with type 1 diabetes, I certainly had more than that one hypoglycemic episode. That is why my mother would insist on being everywhere with me.

Her constant presence fed my extreme need for independence. It also fueled my need to show up in spite of the setbacks and perform. I moved past the fear and shame and did what I had to do to feel fulfilled.

I was implementing Step Four of my Victory Dance even as a young child. While most kids were busy with play dates and Barbie dolls, I was practicing my baton twirling until I made it to the national championships.

When I finally realized dance was my heart and soul, I went at it with all that I had inside me. I had the courage to dispel everyone's doubts and giggles about how serious I was.

I was extremely focused at a young age on moving my life forward. I was intent that my abilities would eventually outshine my limitations, as well as the fact that I had a mentally ill mother whose erratic behavior was often the talk of the community.

While I was deeply afraid of my disease, I was also well aware that time was of the essence and I better not waste any of it. I had the choice to slink back in fear, or push ahead in spite of the fear and make the most of every opportunity.

I chose the latter.

That choice followed me into adulthood. Yes, much of my actions have been rooted in fear. But if courage is feeling the fear and moving ahead regardless, then that has been my natural instinct for as long as I can remember.

I felt unfairly labeled from such a young age, and so I rebelled. What kid wouldn't? This book is about keeping it real.

The flip side is I tackled every obstacle head on and simply kept moving.

The ability to navigate life with diabetes and a mentally ill mother was courage in and of itself.

CHAPTER 17
Transforming Your Poverty Mindset

IN THE TWO YEARS prior to my bus accident, I had made more strides than ever to become a better, stronger, and more courageous version of myself. I had finally grown up. I was very much an adult according to the year I was born, but up until that point, I had not taken responsibility for my life.

Allow me to explain. I grew up with significant means. As a child, there was no lack of external abundance in my crazy little world. I lived in a huge house on the intercoastal in South Florida. I had a huge room with pink everything—a pink canopy bed, pink chair, pink rug, and a closet so full of clothes that I could wear a different outfit to school every day for a month.

Part of my mother's mental illness manifested itself in her daughters, and specifically in us having to look prim and proper at all times. We had to keep up with the Joneses. My parents also tried to coerce me into going to cotillions and becoming a debutante, but I wouldn't have any of it.

We were raised Jewish, but I always felt it was more for show than for spiritual purposes. I went to Sunday school strictly for the snacks. My diabetes "cheating" was in full force, even in elementary school.

I had a Bat Mitzvah, where I wore a fluffy purple dress and spent as much time as I could in the lobby, far away from the festivities. From what I saw, the Bat Mitzvah was just a social event. Since I felt alienated at school and had few friends, all the people in attendance seemed to come at my parents' insistence.

None of it made sense to me. What did make sense is I could have whatever I wanted. I was spoiled, and on some level, I felt the "stuff" made up for my sickness. We had closets full of toys that had never been opened. I definitely did not understand having to work for things, nor did I grasp the value of a dollar.

My parents separated when I was sixteen, and I soon found myself at the center of a brutal alimony fight. I see now my father must have been under amazing pressure to try to keep our lifestyle the same while keeping my mother's unruly financial demands met.

Thanks to her mental illness, she believed he had millions of dollars hidden away in a foreign bank account. Sadly, she spent a lot of time, energy, and money trying to get to this hidden (and totally fabricated) fortune.

Over the next few years, I watched the family financial situation dissolve and the debt increase. But rather than changing our lifestyle, we just kept spending. I was buried so deep in my problems (and so busy chasing my independence) that I missed all the warning signs.

As a result of this dysfunctional relationship with money, I had no idea how to manage any income I made, how to balance a checkbook, or how to set and adhere to a budget. I mumbled about "wanting to work," but my father insisted he could cover

The 'Bat Mitzvah' Dress

my living expenses. Whenever I went to the bank, money was there. Dad would always send me more, so what did I have to worry about?

At the same time, I was overwrought with guilt and shame. I felt like I was living a huge lie, and I was secretly envious of people doing it on their own.

So This Is What Rock Bottom Looks Like

After high school, I essentially ran away to New York City. I should not have been allowed to go to New York in the first place—I was about as far from being a responsible adult as it gets.

My starving and binge dieting had turned to severe binging and laxative abuse. I am still amazed I never went into a high-blood-sugar-induced coma. What's really amazing is that I survived that period at all.

The move to Los Angeles in January 1989 was another representation of having no financial boundaries. I went to visit LA on a whim in fall 1988 and put the entire trip on my dad's credit card. We never discussed it.

Then on another whim, I decided I needed to live in LA because I missed driving and wanted to more effectively pursue my dance dreams. I was already studying at STEPS, a professional dance school in New York City, but I convinced myself my dream could only be fulfilled in LA—and it didn't matter that I'd be walking away from my education.

In the addiction recovery process, they often speak of what's called a "geographic." Simply put, it is when you move to a new city or change your environment in an attempt to change your life. That could have worked, except that when I moved, I took my bad habits, my eating disorder, and my out-of-control lifestyle with me.

My dad continued to support my now-increased living

expenses and my bad habits. When the first rent payment came due, I didn't even know it had to be paid at the beginning of the month. I thought it was paid the day you signed the lease, and that was it!

I realized my father would not be able to pay the tuition at my new college AND all my other expenses. So, I got a minimum wage job at a department store. However, I was too insecure and ashamed of my weight to audition for any real dance work.

After I was forced to give up the keys to my car, that new disability afforded me an even bigger excuse for not working full time. During this period, I frequently sabotaged my success out of fear that I would actually succeed.

When I arrived back in New York City in 2002, the pattern continued, except I no longer had the support of my dad's credit card.

I remember one night a friend had gotten me a job as a bathroom attendant in a downtown club. I spent the night handing drunken women paper towels and hoping they would tip me. I left at 3 a.m. with thirty-three dollars in my pocket. I cried on the way home knowing I'd be able to buy some groceries the next day.

I had such little value for my life that I could not even keep myself fed. I had grown up as the princess. I was the trophy child. I was supposed to be a star. What had happened to me?

Something big needed to change and fast. I knew it was my mindset and overall attitude about life that had caused my financial suffering. I was teetering on the precipice of homelessness. It was now or never.

Admitting there is a problem is the first step toward changing anything. On the advice of a friend, I made a determination to eradicate my "mental poverty." I was always in panic mode, scared of where the next dollar would come from, and yet so flippant and careless with the few dollars I did have.

I've always been such a walking contradiction. I wanted to appear brave, but I was afraid of almost everything. I had a fear of committing to people, goals, job opportunities—you name it. I was afraid to take any kind of real job. I was afraid to date. I feared the wrath of diabetes.

I was also battling tremendous arrogance and deep-seated anger. Part of me felt entitled as a result of my diabetes and the loss of my sight. I felt the world owed me a break.

I masked all that fear with big goals and dreams that gave me a purpose, even though I knew deep down they would never materialize. I was like a dog chasing its tail.

Finally in 2007, I was tired of it all and ready to face life with my big girl pants on. I decided to challenge myself to fully accept my situation and then take action in order to transform. I was, after all, thirty-eight years old.

It was time.

I began reading about financially successful people. What did they do? What habits and actions did they embrace on a regular basis? I started writing down goals and trying to figure out ways to take the right action to make them happen.

I couldn't dance anymore. So what? It was time to stop wallowing in self-pity and being afraid of my own shadow—and instead get down to the business of growing the hell up.

Going Full Throttle

I decided to pursue a residential real estate license on the advice of my friend Tom. I remember him saying to me, "You are good with research and people. I think you will do well."

This was a great suggestion, except that I didn't even have the three hundred dollars to register for the course. I scraped the funds together, and a few weeks later I sat down in the front row of the New York Real Estate Academy. It felt good to be in a new environment and learning a new skill. This was by no means my dream job, but I was determined to move ahead.

Since I was broke, I decided to accelerate the learning schedule and finish all the classes in two weeks. I had never attempted such an ambitious timeline for anything. In college I had broken up my schedule so I'd never have to take on too much at once.

Not this time. I went in full throttle, from 9 a.m. to 6 p.m., seven days a week.

I registered to take the New York State Real Estate exam, but I kept it a secret from almost everyone. I also decided not to make any mention of my visual impairment or diabetes. If this was going to be a truly fresh start, I didn't want my labels coming along for the ride. I wanted people to view me for who I was and not what was wrong with me.

I soon discovered I had walked into a bit of strange community. Many of my fellow students believed that working in New York City real estate was essentially a get-rich-quick scheme. Not me—I had no grand illusions. I knew I was getting into a career that would require the same blood, sweat, and tears it takes to be successful in any profession.

As we neared the end of our classes, directors from various New York City real estate offices came to pitch their firms to the new students. Some promised lofty gains of up to five hundred thousand in the first year, while others were more realistic in presenting the workload and earning potential. The entire process intrigued me.

Some firms were small and had limited resources. Others were massive with hundreds of employees and comprehensive training and support programs. I narrowed it down to three companies. One was a small start-up company, and the other two were among the largest residential real estate firms in the city.

My hard work paid off, and I passed the exam on the first take. This was shocking, as I had always been a poor test taker.

It was also a big confidence booster. It turns out that if I really did put my mind to something, I could make it happen.

That was a first for me.

I interviewed with all three firms—and to my surprise I was given offers in all of them. To clarify, interviewing for a job in residential real estate in New York City is not like interviewing for a standard nine-to-five job. New agents are hired as independent contractors under the support umbrella of the company.

You basically start your own business inside a business. There's no cushy salary or paid vacation time. This also means assuming business costs before you ever start making any money.

I decided to go with New York City's biggest residential firm. While the commission per deal was slightly less, they had an extensive training and support system, and they had offices where I could have my own workspace without any additional expense.

The choreographer, leader, and dancer in me was feeling slightly defeated, but I was also relieved to be blazing a new path. I completed my weeklong training program on Friday afternoon, and while the other trainees went off to celebrate and unwind, I went straight to my new office to get to work.

Didn't See That Coming

My excitement and resolve could not totally make up for some unanticipated drawbacks. I had trouble seeing the numbers on the buildings I showed to clients. I struggled to get the keys into locks. Hallways were dark and steps on buildings were seldom clearly marked, so I found myself tripping a lot.

I did not care. I was determined to be successful. I also decided not to mention either my diabetes or my visual impairment to my manager or any of my coworkers. My new manager supported me in my excitement, and I did not want to see his eyes fill with pity or concern.

My dancer's determination and work ethic was immediately put to good use. I arrived at the office first thing every morning before anyone else arrived. *This is a business*, I thought. *I can't stroll in at 10 or 11 a.m. and expect to be successful.*

In the first weeks of starting my new real estate business, I was also offered a thirty-hour-per-week job as a group fitness manager. The position was in a gym where I had been teaching part-time fitness classes for years.

Tom encouraged me to do both, and so I went for it. The salary from the management job would finally give me enough base income to cover my bottom-line expenses in my real estate business. The real estate commissions would be an added bonus and allow me to start saving.

I knew the pace would be exhausting, but I was ready to change my life for the better. I was ready to expand my capacity in ways I had never imagined possible. I was feeling more courageous than ever before—and it was time to see just what I could do when I truly set my mind to it.

CHAPTER 18
Give Yourself Some Credit

HOW MANY JOBS HAVE you ever had at once? Most of the people I know have had at least two at some point in their lives. If you've ever held down two or more jobs at the same time, then you probably know what I figured out pretty quickly.

Neither of them gets your full attention.

I wanted to be a really successful real estate agent, but given the basic laws of time and space, there was a limit to how much I could get done. So I decided I'd just have to figure out a way to do *more* real estate work in *less* time.

In short, I'd have to become a time management ninja.

Fortunately the gym where I managed was a short bus ride from both my office and my apartment. I worked nights in the gym and the occasional weekend and holiday. That enabled me to get to my real estate office first thing in the morning. I'd work nonstop all day until I had to go to the gym in the evening.

I made back-to-back client appointments and I found myself traveling all over New York City. I was walking up to one hundred blocks per day and climbing countless flights of stairs in walk-up buildings.

In my first few months in real estate I showed lower priced apartments outside my own neighborhood. One day, two things dawned on me. First, why was I going so far away to do my job when I could do it just as well in closer proximity?

Secondly, I realized that I was just as competent as anyone else. Why couldn't I do the big five-figure-a-month deals? I didn't have to only chase the low-hanging fruit. I didn't have to work myself into the ground on small transactions.

I went forth boldly and courageously to chase the bigger fish, and as I took Step Four of my Victory Dance, my confidence grew. I was taking a dramatic turn to better my life, and I'd never felt more happy or fulfilled.

Label-Free Amy

I had yet to mention any of my physical challenges to my new colleagues. I got a strange thrill out of not having anyone know about my disease or visual impairment. For the first time in my life, I felt like I was being accepted on my terms.

I figured out subtle ways to work around my vision problems. I carried a flashlight. I became skilled at quickly feeling for keyholes. I mastered the art of casually stopping to chat with clients to give myself a chance to slow down and avoid tripping over unmarked steps.

I was disappointed at how surprisingly nonaccessible New York City was for those with visual impairments. This was the most engaged I had ever been with the city, and I was shocked and saddened by how difficult it was for me to safely navigate the streets and buildings. This detail would become even more prevalent after my accident while I was wheelchair and walker bound.

Cleverly managing my diabetes also became an interesting challenge. I often found myself out with clients when I needed to test my glucose or take an insulin shot. Sometimes I would get busy and forget to take care of myself, and my diabetes would get out of control. To remedy this, I carried glucose tablets with me everywhere I went. If I felt a hypoglycemic reaction coming on I discreetly popped a few.

I got myself into a rhythm—I worked on real estate from 7 a.m. to 4 p.m. Then I'd go straight to the gym to work until 9:30 p.m. I would arrive home by 10 p.m. and spend another hour or two working on real estate paperwork, setting up appointments, and finalizing deals. I'd be done with that and in bed by midnight. Then I'd wake up at 5 a.m. to start the process all over again.

My new 18-hour workday was exhausting, but the effort was worth it. In an office meeting after my first month in real estate, my manager called me out to praise my work and focus. She held up an impressive stack of deal applications I had already submitted. "Amy has only been here a month. What's happening with the rest of you? She even has a second full-time job."

I wasn't trying to impress anyone. I was just trying to transform my financial situation and prove to myself I could get the job done. I wasn't there to make friends or hang out and drink coffee. I was there to work, and since my time was limited by my other job I did not have a minute to spare.

I simply got up and went to work. I kept telling myself it did not have to be forever. There was something so incredibly liberating about taking charge of my own life. It was hard—but I knew about "hard." I also knew if I set my mind to something I could make it happen almost instantaneously.

And the Award Goes to . . .

Winter hit hard that first year in real estate, but I kept moving. I was determined to see myself on the company's top producers list every single month. To accomplish this an agent had to close five deals before month's end. Game on! I am highly competitive and enjoyed the challenge.

By the spring, I was beginning to feel the wear and tear on

my body and the fatigue from the hours I was keeping. I had little to no social life and zero creative outlets. The upshot is my financial life had stabilized. I found that I was cautious with my earnings, probably because of being broke for so long. I repaired my credit, was current on all bills, and had even started saving money.

I had started my real estate business in November 2007. At the end of my first year in December 2008, the company executives came to visit our office. Much to my shock and surprise I was awarded the Rookie of the Year award for new agents. That Rookie of the Year award sits on my shelf to this day. It is one of my life accomplishments for which I am most proud.

Over the first year, I made new friends and learned a lot about the real estate world and how deceitful people can be in the hustle. I had gained a reputation for being trustworthy and really knowing my products and client needs. I was building a strong clientele based purely on my hard work, diligence, and honesty.

I put my head down and went to work, and it paid off in so many ways. I implemented Step Four of my Victory Dance and acted with courage. I challenged my visual impairment, my diabetes, and an unbelievable schedule—and I was victorious.

I could have let myself remain stuck. I could have kept trying to teach dance and fitness classes on the side and barely make ends meet.

In SGI Nichiren Buddhism there is an idea that if you want to understand the effects of your life today, look at the causes you have made in the past. I had been making very weak causes based on fear and a lack of belief in my ability and power.

I simply started making new causes. Was it tough? Of course. But what did I do? I kept moving. Having the courage to look wholeheartedly at my life and realize that something had to change was the turning point for me.

As I started my second official year as a New York City

residential real estate agent, I now had something amazing—I had choices. Being out of debt and earning a decent income for the first time in my adult life was one of my most amazing and empowering achievements.

By late winter 2008 I began exploring my options for next steps. I was considering graduate school in production and management. While I still loved dancing and taking and teaching classes, I had also grown fascinated with the behind-the-scenes process of producing concert and theatrical work.

I was starting to miss my creative work. I was also extremely tired from having two full time jobs. I began to have conversations with my managers at the gym about taking on a bigger managerial role and phasing down my time as a real estate agent. I felt confident—for the first time ever—that I could accomplish whatever I set my mind to do.

On the morning of May 1, 2009, after a long and cold winter, I remember thinking that it was finally glorious springtime. My heart felt lighter, and I was more hopeful than I had been in a long time about my future. I had just started a new part-time gig helping to produce and choreograph a dance production. I had a full day of real estate related meetings scheduled and then planned to go to the gym to finish the instructor payroll for the upcoming pay period.

Life changes in an instant.

Little did I know when I left the house that morning I would not come home for four months. Little did I know that I would soon find myself pinned under the tire of a fifteen-ton bus.

Little did I know I would continue in unseen and previously unfathomable ways to ignite Step Four of my Victory Dance. I had proven to myself it was possible, and now the stakes were about to get even higher.

CHAPTER 19
Fake It Till You Make It

THE MONTHS FOLLOWING MY successful settlement agreement were pure insanity. New York City Transit had ninety days to turn over the funds. Even this got delayed. I was amazed at how they seemed to have no problem paying out interest for late payment rather than just handing over the goods. Some things I just didn't understand.

I was still getting by on the kindness of friends, but at least now I knew I'd be able to pay everyone back in the near future.

I began to think about what I wanted life to look like now that I did not have a legal case hanging over my head. While my body had been rebuilt, I had put very little energy into building a new identity to go along with it. I had been focusing for almost five years on just staying alive. Suddenly here came that question I'd been able to avoid all this time: *Now what?*

I hadn't thought much about dancing. I had blocked that part of my brain from being able to contribute to my thought process. I just knew I wanted to get back to work doing something. Anything. But while I was somewhat physically stronger, I had a lot of work to do to compensate for the massive structural damage in my newly reassembled leg.

I was being medicated for my post-traumatic stress disorder, but social situations were still uncomfortable. And what about being deformed? How did I feel about that? I struggled so deeply my entire life in the romantic arena, and now on top of everything else, I had this deformed right leg. My solution was just not to think about it. I'd figure that one out later.

Are You In Or Not?

In my neighborhood travels I kept running into another dancer. She was a beautiful, tall, model-thin young woman who also walked with a limp. We regularly struck up conversations on the bus or in the gym. She had suffered a traumatic brain injury and, like me, she had been told she would not survive.

That never stopped her from dancing. She had recently choreographed a series of ballets. She also kept prodding me to come to a dance class.

"No," I'd say each time she asked. "I can't dance anymore."

Over the next few months we began chatting about collaborating on a show. She was getting ready to showcase some new work and wanted to know if I cared to contribute.

"A show? A dance show?" I asked. The words sounded foreign on my lips.

I kept brushing her off, never giving a firm answer either way. "We'll see," I'd say, hoping she would take the hint and stop asking.

I had no idea where the dance part of me fit in my new life. As far as I was concerned that part was gone. I had been crushed and managed to stay alive. But now I needed to find something else to do.

My new friend finally demanded an answer. "Are you in or not? Because I want to start working on new choreography."

Despite my best efforts, I said yes. When I did, something amazing happened. The dancer and producer in me awoke from a deep sleep. My mind went crazy. Where, when, how, location, date, details—there were so many details.

It was late February 2014, and my settlement was still in turn around. *This is going to cost money*, I thought. *As of right now, I don't have any. But I will soon.* I had always dreamed of being able to produce artistic work and actually pay dancers their worth. Maybe this would be the start.

We decided to move forward with our show.

"What are we going to do?" she asked.

"I have no idea."

As with every decision in my life I started with my spiritual base, chanting "Nam Myoho Renge Kyo." I also mentioned my plan to a friend who was a cast member of *The Lion King* on Broadway. He suggested I reach out to his friend, a seasoned dancer named Ricardo.

When I Googled Ricardo, I almost fell out of my chair. He was AMAZING and had an impressive resume filled Broadway credits, commercial work, and tenures with both classical and modern dance companies.

I emailed Ricardo about the potential show dates and mentioned our mutual friend. He responded that he was interested and possibly available.

My producing friend and I decided to host an official audition. We set a performance date in May that just so happened to be my forty-fifth birthday. It was also the anniversary month of my accident. It was a big month.

I had not danced in over five years. *Wow, can I really do this?* Inside I was terrified, but on the outside I was living Step Four of my Victory Dance. I found the courage to forge ahead.

Do They Know I've Never Done This Before?

We got a good response to the audition, especially considering it was a first-time job for a group with no reputation. Since I was not able to dance, I enlisted the help of my dancer friend James who was then on injury hiatus from the Broadway musical *The Lion King*. He would teach the choreography at the auditions. This meant I had to get back in the studio and create something to teach.

I came up with two different styles of choreography based on my background as a classically trained dancer. We chose to focus on ballet and lyrical contemporary dance, which had always been my passion.

Audition day arrived, and I was so nervous. When I got to the studio, seven dancers were warming up in the hallway. One of the dancers was a top-ten finalist from a season of the hit reality show *So You Think You Can Dance*.

I felt like such a fraud. Did they know I had never done this? Did they know this was our inaugural performance? Did they know I could not even dance?

I put all my fears aside, and like I had done at so many other times in my life, I showed up with a confident smile. Before we started, I briefly explained the goal of the performance and how I had arrived at this moment. I encouraged the dancers to just dance from their hearts. Little did I know I was setting up the forum for what would become a serious professional dance company.

James did an amazing job of teaching the choreography, and I quickly learned the vocabulary to express what I wanted as a director without actually being able to demonstrate the movement.

It was one of the most amazing days I had experienced since my accident. It was a day that gave me the sense that literally step by step, I'd be able to make something of my life after all.

I hired all of the attendees but one. Over the next few weeks, more amazing dancers were referred to my performance. There was Ricardo; my friend Rosie from the cast of *In the Heights*; Florient (aka Flo), winner of *You Can Dance* (France's franchise of *So You Think You Can Dance*); members of The Alvin Ailey American Dance Theater; graduates of the Juilliard School of Dance; and members of Dance Theater of Harlem.

I suddenly felt like I was in a dream rather than a nightmare. I had planned to create just one or two sections of choreography. The more amazing the dancers, the more I found myself wanting to build.

As producers, my friend and I both wanted our stories to inspire hope in others. So we decided to offer a panel discussion after the performance. The panel would be comprised of our mutual treatment teams. Two of my surgeons agreed to speak on how they help patients overcome trauma as severe as mine.

I completely immersed myself in the production process. What had started as simple choreography for two sections quickly morphed into an opening production number followed by a full-length contemporary ballet.

I was being forced to expand my life—creatively, socially, physically, emotionally, and spiritually. It was admittedly a bit of a haphazard process, but since time was short, I could not overthink things.

As the date drew near, we were scheduled to rehearse the big finale. Rehearsal wasn't even supposed to start until 8 p.m., but I had felt overwhelmingly fatigued and sick all day. I had already pushed myself past the limits I thought my leg could go, and I had little left to give.

The dancers came in one by one. I stood at the stereo looking at some of the most seasoned dancers in the world. I swallowed hard, holding back tears of amazement. At the same time, I was literally dizzy with fatigue.

Do these artists know how bad I am feeling right now? They stood in their places patiently waiting for *my* direction. I was gasping inside.

Rehearsal began, and I found the strength. It was so inspiring to watch them move. In my heart I was dancing right along with them. More than that, I was living out Step Four of my Victory Dance.

I felt the fear, the pain, and the doubt, and showed up anyway.

We Need More Chairs

This little party we had first planned was growing by the day. We covered our social media pages with announcements about this amazing company of dancers that would be performing on my forty-fifth birthday.

My anxiety was mounting as all the moving parts started turning. We decided to host the event at the esteemed Alvin Ailey Center for Dance in New York City. We were preselling tickets like crazy. I had to ask the building to give us a bigger space.

The irony was that I was still borrowing money to survive and living in a tiny, overcrowded room. I was literally figuring things out as I went along. I had gone from asking myself "What now?" to scheduling rehearsals for five different sections of choreography. I was also marketing and handling all the event details.

My savior, Andy, again came to the rescue in early May 2014. Since my settlement deal with New York City Transit was signed and in process, he secured a significant temporary loan against my case. The money came through the second week of May.

Suddenly the floodgates opened. Just like that I was building a dream that had been dormant since I was pinned under the tire of that fifteen-ton bus five years earlier. I got my own big-girl apartment and was genuinely filled with hope for the future, maybe for the first time since that fateful day.

The performance day arrived. My father, nephew, sister, and brother-in-law came in for the show. Andy and Dr. Spector and Dr. Yaghoobzadeh were also in attendance. In just two months, we had created a full ballet and new production number to open the show, which was entitled "Human Revolution."

When we had been discussing a title for the show I blurted out, "The Victory Dance Project." And so the mission was born.

The house opened thirty-five minutes before curtain. I stood in the doorway, eyes filled with tears of amazement at everything going on around me. I kept thinking of that moment in the ambulance when I had chanted "Victory Dance." I had done it—I manifested this glorious endeavor out of extreme tragedy.

My moment was sharply interrupted.

"Amy, we need you."

It was my friend Alyse who was taking tickets at the door.

"What's wrong?" I asked her.

"We are oversold and people are still coming. How many can we hold in the space? Can you delay the start time a few minutes so we can get more chairs?"

We ended up with a standing-room-only crowd of nearly two hundred people. Whatever was happening, it was bigger than all of us.

The show went off without a hitch. While there were some hiccups in the choreography, the heart and soul came through with resounding spirit. The standing ovation went on for an extended period of time. It was surreal.

People who had known me for years looked at me dumbfounded and remarked, "I had no idea you did this."

"Neither did I," was my reply.

As I was having coffee with my family on the morning after the performance, a woman walked up to me. "I was at the performance last night," she gushed. "Wow, I am still so moved.

My heart is so full. It was perhaps the most moving and inspiring thing I have ever seen."

I thanked her. I was still amazed and overwhelmed we had pulled it off and landed a standing-room-only crowd. I was also exhausted and in the midst of moving for the third time in seven months.

I feel sometimes we think of *courage* as this big, auspicious ideal. I think it's much simpler than that. I believe courage comes from simply facing and moving through whatever it is that is right in front of us. It is not necessarily producing a show with world-class dancers, starting a business, or running for office. It is simply being truthful to ourselves and knowing that whatever doubt and discord we are feeling is not only OK, it is also normal and to be expected.

I see courage every day in the smallest of actions.

I still get nervous about heading into rehearsal or setting new choreography. The fear, doubt, and uncertainty come along for the ride. But Step Four of the Victory Dance continues to remind and reinforce the power of showing up and doing it anyway.

It may be painful, and it may take longer than expected, but this step is crucial to creating your most glorious Victory Dance. Congratulations! You have now moved through Step Four. You are now in the home stretch.

'Standing Ovation'

Step Five
Enthusiasm

CHAPTER 20
Inspired By Kim K.

WE HAVE REACHED THE final step, but our dance is far from over. The five steps are like every move we take in life: Sometimes we walk with strength. Other times we stumble. Sometimes our determination and courage come easily. Other times they seem to falter.

There will be days, maybe even months or years, when it may be hard to accept what has happened to you or around you. The one constant for those of us who find our personal Victory Dance is that we never give up. We Just. Keep. Moving.

No one says you have to do this with a fake smile pasted on your face, but for what it's worth, I have found that smiling through the pain makes it more bearable. After a while, the enthusiasm becomes ingrained, almost like a habit. If that sounds too good to be true, stay with me. I'll explain how enthusiasm can become a part of your dance—every step of the way.

An Unlikely Source of Inspiration

After our very first standing-room-only performance at the Alvin Ailey Center for Dance, I took a step back and had some important revelations. For starters, I discovered that even though I was financially stable and had once again found my place in the world of dance, there was still so much about my life and my direction that was uncertain.

More importantly, I saw that even though it looked like things had "all worked out" on the surface, I was still feeling extreme inner turmoil. I was no longer scraping together pennies for my next meal, and I had created value out of a horrible circumstance. Yet I was still not approaching life with any sincere enthusiasm.

I began to wonder if that was even possible.

After such a successful and well-received first performance, we decided to plan a one-year anniversary show set to take place in summer 2015. For those who knew me during that time, it is no secret that the anniversary performance was a tumultuous production that took a tremendous toll on me.

The experience wasn't entirely negative. We awarded our first annual "Artist for Peace" award to Renee Robinson, a legendary principal dancer with the Alvin Ailey American Dance Theater. There were other far less amazing things about the experience, and while we had pulled it off, the whole process left me angry and frustrated.

I was still growing into my role as "The Boss." Even worse, I tried to be all things to all people. Boundaries and difficult conversations were never my forte, so when I found myself working with a few insecure and ego-driven artists, I essentially hid in my apartment to let everything sort itself out. Imagine my surprise when my foolproof conflict-resolution plan fell flat.

As usual, my eyes were also bigger than my stomach. Even though I had long since let go of my rock star career aspirations, whenever I started a new project, Madonna's *Truth or Dare* was my benchmark. That was the bar I had set for myself, and I didn't feel like we were measuring up at all. At one point in the process, I made the mistake of unloading my frustration onto a colleague, who asked, "Do you have to set your standards so high?"

This infuriated me even more. *Yes*, I thought. *YES I do!*

I took a break after that show to figure out what I wanted. Now that my case was settled and the emergent medical situations seemed to be less frequent, a strange void formed where all the drama once lived. I was feeling directionless. I kept chanting, but I had no idea what to do next.

I felt a staggering amount of guilt over my sudden financial security, and I also spent a significant amount of emotional energy combatting everyone else's reaction to my financial windfall.

Unfortunately, as it turns out, a comfortable bank account is not a cure for severe depression. Who knew? And while I had become quite the expert at putting on a perky face in public, as soon as I got home, I put on my sweats and hit the couch, ready to forget I was part of the human race for a few hours. My fear of gaining weight kept me working out, but otherwise, I was utterly devoid of all motivation.

While lying on the couch channel surfing one evening, I came across an episode of *Keeping Up with the Kardashians*. As I watched in amazement, something in me snapped. I am sure they are lovely people, but I thought, *Wow, if Kim K. and her entourage can gain this big a platform, then I can certainly work to build an empire that will be a useful and positive force in the world.*

I have to hand it to the Kardashian clan: they are brilliant marketers.

I stood up and started to chant. A couple minutes later, I started scrolling through my Facebook feed and came across a post for a seminar in Los Angeles for people who wanted to be motivational speakers.

I'm not usually a sucker for seminars, but something about this struck me. All of the featured speakers were people I knew and respected in the entertainment industry. On an impulse, I started to register.

A moment later, I deleted the registration.

No way, I thought. *You are not seriously considering flying across the country to spend a week with a bunch of people you don't know.*

I kept chanting. Something drew me back to my laptop. I quelled the negative voice in my head with a simple and decisive, "YES, I AM." I had the miles to pay for the flight and friends to see in Los Angeles.

This would be the biggest trip I would attempt since my accident. It had also been ten years since I had set foot on California soil. I had no idea how I would handle the travel, the crowds, the standing, and the meals, but I pressed on and registered as a VIP attendee. A few weeks later, I was headed once again to La La Land.

Let the Awakening Begin

It was December 2015 and the weather in New York was turning colder, so I was happy to spend a week in the sunshine. I traveled to California a few days before the event and visited Santa Monica, my former home. I was incredibly nervous about this new adventure, but as I had always done—I just kept moving.

I arrived at registration the night before the conference began and encountered a long check-in line at the huge hotel where the conference was being held. *Here we go. Obstacle number one.*

I was working hard to blend myself back into normal life, and I did not want to be known as "the girl with the deformed leg" at the event. But I also couldn't stand for more than a few minutes at a time.

I really didn't have much choice, so I found someone working with the event and pulled him aside. In my usual sarcastic tone, I explained I had a "disability" and joked about being run over by a bus (because who wouldn't find that funny?). The entire event staff was extremely supportive throughout the event, and I was deeply grateful.

The creator of the boot camp, James Malinchak, is a highly respected speaker and business coach. James was featured on the hit ABC series *Secret Millionaire*. As I listened to James talk the first day, it was like all the information I had been missing on how to build a successful business was right there in front of me. When James offered one-on-one coaching, I immediately filled out an application.

It was four days of information overload. It was also four days of managing my diabetes and pain away from home. By the final day, I had to go up to my room to sleep during much of the morning session. I decided to cut myself some slack. All things considered, I had accomplished so much just by being willing to step outside my comfort zone.

Even with the pain, I knew that this was where my life needed to be. I was relieved to find myself in a new community of business-minded entrepreneurs. Being whisked out of my environment shed new light on my life. I found myself sharing, connecting, and being *FEARLESS*! It was as if that depressed and isolated person who spent her nights channel surfing just a few weeks earlier had drifted out to sea.

Not long after I got home to New York, I got a call from James's office saying my application had been accepted for his coaching program. This was the sharp right turn I didn't even know I needed! I had been whisked out of my trauma-filled life and into the glorious world of possibilities. I was told and encouraged that I could do anything. Even better than that, I was acquiring the business tools and relationships necessary to make it happen.

Reigniting the Mission

As 2016 rolled along, my frequent flyer miles went through the roof. I took seminars on brain-based learning, speaking, media training, and how to pitch products. I felt like I was in business school. As with everything I have done in my life, I went at this new series of tasks with full intensity. If I was going to do something, I had to do it all the way.

My approach to my work and my life was changing. I was also realizing that I had everything it took to be a successful speaker, coach, and author. The only difference between those who were succeeding and me was that they manifested opportunities, got hired, and did the work. I traveled to Los Angeles every few months. In the midst of my cross-country trips, the Victory Dance Project had been accepted into a choreography festival in spring 2016 for a twenty-minute spot. This would be my first venture back to my new dance life since encountering the many obstacles of the one-year anniversary performance in 2015.

I determined to approach it differently, so I started thinking about it like a business (as I should have been doing all along). How can I serve the audience? What makes me different? How can we better market not only the level of the work, but also our true mission?

We held an audition to bring some fresh energy to the company. Much to my surprise, seventy-nine dancers attended, and we hired five. I also hired some business and administrative support so I did not have to manage every last detail.

I made my expectations crystal clear to my new dancers and staff members. I realized that laying the framework ahead of time would circumvent the personality and organizational problems we had experienced in the past. Can you believe it? I was finally learning from my mistakes!

It was during this time that we began to entertain the idea of doing a three-year anniversary show, as well as a documentary film about my "journey of movement." I also determined to wrap up this book. Everyone said it would take years, but I had other plans. Now that I had battled the bus and won, I could use it all to create value—and I was more than ready to share this message with the world.

All I Do Is Win

The expansion of my realm continued. I found myself surrounded by some of the leading business and marketing minds on the planet. Everyone I met reacted with such sincere support and praise of my mission. The overachiever in me was on fire.

One year later, in December 2016, I returned to the same seminar that had so dramatically impacted my life. However, this time I found myself on the stage as a nominee for the "Marketer of the Year" award. On the morning of the competition, I chanted for every single person to be encouraged and that hearts would be moved by my story. The audience sprung to its feet at the end of my presentation. I was overwhelmed by the response from simply and sincerely sharing my experiences.

The combination of preparation and prayer must have worked because I WON the award! In twelve short months, my life had been transformed in ways I could never have imagined. I was still battling depression, but the bouts were shorter and becoming less frequent. I had literally *moved* my way into a new world full of possibility and success. Little did I know that some of my most affirming and transformative moments were just around the corner.

Through my determination and actions, I had created

enthusiasm where there was none. The dance was still in progress, but it was making more sense. I felt like I had been given permission to succeed rather than continuing to be held back by other people's (and my own) perceived limitations.

Part of me still felt like a huge fraud, but I was starting to pile up experiences, tangible accolades, and support that were slowly canceling out the little voices in my head. I felt an enthusiasm for life I had literally never felt before. There was still work to do, but I was feeling bolder and bolder each day.

And why not? I put myself at center stage and literally won!

With James Malinchak: Business coach & star of the Hit ABC TV Show 'America's Secret Millionaire'

I won! Marketer of the Year

CHAPTER 21
Learning from Our Mistakes

HAVE YOU EVER SWORN something off forever? It never works, does it? Especially not when it's something you love.

Well, I love dance. I also love producing. So, when I swore off any further work with the Victory Dance Project after our tumultuous one-year anniversary performance, I knew I'd never stay away forever.

It had been a wholly exhausting pursuit, and I wasn't sure I'd ever be able or willing to do it again. Still, something kept pulling me back, even though I had been moving my life in drastically new directions. Choreographing and producing was simply what I knew. It felt like home.

Always needing to top myself, I decided our three-year anniversary performance would be bigger and better. My business director and I put together a timeline and figured out what kind of support we would need to pull this thing off in a bold, life-changing way. The event space was confirmed for June 15, 2017, which was seven months away. That seemed like plenty of time but also way too soon.

In late 2016, we began inviting potential award recipients

for our "Woman of Valor" and "Artist for Peace" awards, which were created to honor amazing trailblazers in the world of dance and entertainment. We were also in full swing filming for the documentary. I had agreed to dance in the upcoming performance, so we decided to document my return to the stage after such a traumatic accident.

While I am not a fan of being in front of the camera, I felt the movie would be a source of hope and encouragement. I wanted to not only chronicle my journey of recovery, but I also wanted to showcase the immense challenges of daily life with diabetes. I also felt it might help others to witness what life looks like as a forty-something, single female entrepreneur facing visible and not so visible disabilities in New York City.

Brian, my film director, had an impressive career as a dancer and choreographer and now photographer and director. His sphere of dance industry influence included an Emmy nomination for choreographing for pop icon Michael Jackson as well as the likes of Broadway and stage icons Liza Minnelli and Chita Rivera. He shot and edited a stunning promo video and sent the promo, a link to our website, and the "Woman of Valor" invitation letter to a well-connected friend who could get the letter into the right hands.

Then we waited.

She Said Yes!

My assistant and I began the overwhelming task of scheduling a full-fledged concert that included twelve sections of choreography with eighteen dancers. While some members of the production team encouraged me to reduce the number of hires, I knew I needed to see some new talent. Audition day came, and we had a full house yet again, with spillover.

Having learned from my past mistakes—and having witnessed firsthand the devastating effects of my chronic niceness—I let everyone know up front exactly what I expected. They had to commit to the rehearsal schedule, stay off their phones (this is even written into my contracts now), and be vested in the bigger mission of the company.

By day's end, we found a few true gems and we added them to our group of existing dancers. And so the whirlwind process began. I was determined to be more organized than ever and prove we were a professional company that could hold our own.

In mid-March, I got a phone call, and a lovely British voice introduced herself as Rosie. "I am Chita Rivera's assistant," she announced.

I almost fell over. Chita Rivera—the Broadway legend, Tony Award-winning actress, dancer, and singer!

She continued. "Chita received your letter and saw your video. She is in New York and would be honored to accept the 'Woman of Valor' Award at the June fifteenth performance."

I fell silent. I was torn between shock, elation, and panic. *Holy shit, what do I do now? Could we pull this off?* I kept my cool. I thanked Rosie and we set a plan to handle the details and make a press announcement.

If I felt the pressure to produce before, the stress was off the charts now. I informed the dancers and let them know that I expected only the highest caliber work. I have learned from so many years of practicing SGI Nichiren Buddhism that when I take on a project of this *magnitude*, I am likely to experience *magnificent* obstacles. This situation was no different. What was different was that I now had a *magnificent* team of people supporting the process—and with each obstacle we created a new answer.

Just Like a Swan

A few months in, rehearsals were going well. What was not going well was my ability to keep up physically on the endless rehearsal days. Chris Jackson, the choreographer for my dance, was extremely mindful of my physical issues. I, on the other hand, was not so mindful. I'd give it everything I had. When the other dancers left, I'd lie down to wait for the pain to diminish enough to move.

As I lay there in agony, I'd say to myself, *"You are nearing fifty years on this earth, you have diabetes, and your body has been rebuilt. Can you cut yourself some slack?"*

The answer was always no.

On the surface, everything seemed to be progressing perfectly, and yet every night I went to bed stricken with panic. Like the swan so beautifully gliding on top of the water while its legs are moving furiously underneath, my outward smiles and laughter distracted from what was really going on inside.

Every email, phone call, and detail was handled. That wasn't the problem anymore. So what was the problem? I was struggling to feel any honest joy in the process. There was no enthusiasm. My whole life felt like a show that demanded me to paste on a good face every time I stepped outside my door.

The deeper into production we got, the further I withdrew. I feared that my reaction to anything in life would be panic. It had been nearly eight years since the accident. I was moving on with my life. Yet I always felt like I was drowning.

On Brian's suggestion, I decided that the gala performance would include a tribute to the heroic efforts of my surgical dream team. New York Presbyterian Weill Cornell Medical Center graciously granted the documentary team permission to interview my surgeons for the documentary and footage to use during the gala.

For the first time I heard my surgeon's' side of the story—and it was not what I expected to hear. I did not know they were still contemplating amputation during my months in intensive care and even in the years after while treating my massive infection.

I did not know they had significant concerns about what type of life I would be able to lead.

Hearing all this made me sink further away.

My true emotions were being held prisoner inside as I felt increasing pressure to keep it all together and stay "inspiring" to the outside world. But I kept showing up. *I don't know,* I thought. *Maybe all my forced enthusiasm will become real if I keep it up long enough.*

Fake it 'til you make it, right?

My physical body was breaking down from the stress and physical demands. On top of the pain I was already managing, I started having serious shoulder issues due to the removal of shoulder muscle from the initial 2009 surgery. An MRI showed a tear in my left rotator cuff. This is an intensely painful injury. I was also having compensatory pain in my left foot.

I wasn't looking to be pain free. I simply wanted the pain levels to go back to normal. My treatment team stepped in and saved the day. I got a cortisone shot for the shoulder pain and had acupuncture for the foot pain. However, after this new series of physical obstacles, I began to ask myself some hard questions.

Am I doing this because I want to, or because I think other people want me to?

How much can my body really take?

Am I in denial of my limitations?

I didn't have the answers yet. However, asking the hard questions finally woke me up, and I determined to stop withdrawing and hiding like some defeated, wounded animal.

I was crushed by a bus and came out dancing on the other side! I had determined to save my leg. Leg saved. I made a commitment to stand behind a podium a few months after being pinned under a bus tire. I stood tall. I determined that New York Transit would do the right thing. I was vindicated.

I really can decide my own future, even though I might not get to choose the unforeseen obstacles I may encounter along the away. I can do whatever I want, which also means I can choose to find enthusiasm in each inch of the journey.

That is when I first started to realize that like acceptance, excitement is a *choice*. It's not something that just comes naturally to most of us. It is absolutely a conscious choice.

There is an inherent discomfort in taking on any new challenge. This is why it is important to keep moving. If one step in the dance is not working, it's OK! Trial and error often yield the best results, but may be painful in the process.

Just remember that enthusiasm and happiness are not some hypothetical destinations you can aspire to "reach" one day. They are found within the journey itself. I can't say I was totally there yet—but I was getting closer.

Broadway Royalty

Amidst all of these musings and revelations, one fact remained—I still had to produce a kick-ass show. The cortisone shot in my shoulder had all but vanished the pain. My blood sugar had come back down to normal after some initial spikes thanks to the cortisone. As much as part of me hated to admit, the excuses for why I couldn't or shouldn't dance were fading away.

In May 2017 my publicist informed me that we had been invited to see Chita Rivera perform her cabaret show at the famous Carlyle Hotel, a classy, old-school New York performance space. I was feeling desperate to be inspired and immediately said yes.

With documentary film crew in tow, we witnessed Chita's breathtaking performance. When you are around the top talent in any industry, it does something to you—like witnessing a master chef prepare a dish, or one of the great artists paint a portrait. Watching a master perform his or her art transports you to another place and time. She was truly a wonder to watch.

After the show, I finally met Rosie and thanked her for all her help. Then it got even better. I saw a man walking toward me in the lobby. It was none other than Mr. Ben Vereen. In the world of Broadway and theater, he is pure royalty. Rosie made the introduction, and Mr. Vereen embraced me with such grace and excitement. It turns out he had also had a near-death accident and subsequently returned to the stage.

Then things became even more surreal, as I was introduced moments later to Chita Rivera. We had a brief exchange and she remarked that she had seen our video and read my story. Awestruck, all I could think to say was, "Thank you." We embraced, and I walked away determined to do her justice on show night. The entire evening felt like an out-of-body experience—but we got it all on film, so I know it was real!

I went back to the first step of my Victory Dance and redetermined to create the most amazing production I could possibly manifest. The enthusiasm in me was literally bubbling over. What had changed other than meeting someone who inspires me? Nothing on the surface—and yet everything inside of me was being transformed.

Not Your Average Dress Rehearsal

My team and I had gone to great lengths to have Ms. Rivera attend the dress rehearsal. We also went to great lengths to keep this a secret from the dancers. At the start of tech week, I bumped up the call time for the dancers' arrival on dress rehearsal day to ensure everyone would be there before Ms. Rivera arrived.

By that time, there were a lot of us—we are talking about eighteen performers, the tech crew, a rehearsal director, the video crew, and my staff. Somehow everyone was in the building when Ms. Rivera arrived almost thirty minutes early. I did my best to stay calm, but I am fairly certain I tripped over my words and talked way too fast. It's not every day that one of your idols comes to watch you perform!

My team pulled all the dancers into the downstairs lobby before her arrival, so they had no idea she was there. The elevator door opened and Saleem, a senior company member, was suddenly standing eye to eye with Chita Rivera. He blushed as I turned to Ms. Rivera and quipped, "Oh, Saleem is my husband for the day."

She burst out laughing. *Chita Rivera thinks I'm funny!*

We came around the stairwell and there was my dance company, the rest of my team, my dad, and a few of my closest friends. They all looked as dumbfounded as I felt.

Soon it was time for the dress rehearsal to begin. Ms. Rivera and I took our seats in the theater as the dancers made their way to the stage wings. When the dancers were ready, the lights went dark and the show began. Toward the end of the opening piece, Ms. Rivera asked, "Who choreographed this? Amy, did you do this?"

"Yes," I replied anxiously.

She replied that she loved my work. *Chita Rivera loves my work!*

We ran the full show, including my performance. At the end, Ms. Rivera leapt to her feet with loud applause. She gushed words of praise and encouragement for our performance. Tears welled up in my eyes but I was somehow able to keep them from streaming down my face.

I wanted to stop and savor the moment, but we still had work to complete before the actual performance, which was set to take place the following evening. I hugged Ms. Rivera and her assistant, Rosie, and our production hats went back on.

When I got home that night, the pain was unreal. As I sat

Broadway Legend & Two Time Tony Award Winner
Chita Rivera at Dress Rehearsal

there, the past eight years played in a loop in my mind. There had been so much agony on all levels. Even though my life had settled on the surface, I still felt such turmoil. And then suddenly, one of my idols is singing my praises. Me—weird, sick Amy! If this wasn't a time to choose to be enthusiastic about life, then I was missing the point!

Just before I went to bed that night, I sent a text message to Gary, my brilliant rehearsal director. It simply said, "That was surreal."

Gary responded, "Yes, it was."

I hate to say it, but for many years, I honestly never thought I'd smile a sincere smile or feel real joy ever again. I was mistaken—and how glad I was to be wrong! This was true victory, pure and simple.

CHAPTER 22
Dancing Because We Can

AFTER ALMOST A YEAR of planning and rehearsing, the day of our three-year anniversary gala and postshow party had arrived. Many special friends and colleagues were attending from all over the country. Janet, my friend from twenty years earlier who had introduced me to the SGI and Nichiren Buddhism, was one of the guests who flew in for the occasion.

I felt an overwhelming sense of responsibility to profoundly impact the audience and to make the travel, cost, and experience worth everyone's while. I felt this pressure even though I knew it's not what Madonna would have felt. One of the scenes that struck me most from *Truth or Dare* involved an exchange in the lobby of Madonna's hotel between Madonna and a childhood friend named Moira. Moira brought Madonna flowers and asked if she could sit down for a moment to chat with the star.

Madonna politely refused and explained that she needed to prepare for the upcoming performance and told her friend, "When you see the show you'll forgive me for not talking to you."

I remember people being offended by this exchange,

thinking that Madonna was being incredibly rude. I understood, though. She had a job to do and she was completely focused on that job and that job only.

As a chronic people pleaser, I was astonished by this act of focus. *Wow,* I thought. *I have never set those kinds of boundaries before.* So the day of the show I took my queue from Madonna and gave myself some space and solitude. I chanted and reflected quietly, determined to create my own *Truth or Dare* moment.

Somebody Pinch Me

I hid myself in the dressing room as the sounds of people filing in grew from a light bustle to a healthy roar. I tried to stay focused, but I began to feel dangerously hypoglycemic. I quickly reached for some candy and glucose tablets, but it was too late—a few moments later, I was on the floor.

C'mon! Do I ever get a break? My face was completely numb, and I lay there waiting for the carbs and sugar to kick in and get me back on my feet. I simultaneously began to feel guilty about how much candy I had just eaten. Then came the weight gain panic. Old habits die hard, I guess.

There I was, about to experience one of the biggest nights of my life. Instead of feeling every ounce of joy in the moment, I was lying on the floor waiting for the feeling in my face to return and panicking over the weight I might gain. This pretty much sums up the immense paradox of my life in general.

My solo dance was halfway through the show.. I was also supposed to give some opening remarks. Unfortunately, my unplanned dressing room floor siesta took whatever time I had left to practice my opener. Now I was feeling really unprepared. I quickly got dressed, feeling fatter and more bloated than ever. But it mattered not. It was time. There was nothing left to do but dance.

Despite my own rocky start to the evening, the entire show was a stunning success. The dancers performed beautifully and had the audience up on its feet before the show was even over. My performance was seamless. The tribute to the hospital was poignant. One of my surgeons, Dr. Bessey, gave some especially moving and humbling remarks.

The "Woman of Valor" presentation to Ms. Rivera was perfection. Our esteemed recipient was outstanding, humble, and sincere. She looked radiant and kicked up her leg in high-heeled shoes like it was nothing—all of this at eighty-four years old.

Everyone was invited to the postshow party, which was complete with a red carpet for photo ops. As we ascended the stairs, people began applauding. We got photos with everyone, and friends kept pulling me aside. It was a strange but exciting experience, as I was torn between feeling fat and excited while the cameras snapped away. I had to force myself to stay present and enjoy such an immense experience.

I spoke again briefly before the party got into full swing. I tried to be the social butterfly I thought I was supposed to be. My shoulder was burning in pain and I had been standing in regular shoes for way too long. Someone brought me a chair and an ice pack, and I gladly sat down. Looking back on that moment, part of me wishes I had been up and schmoozing. What can I say? The introvert in me likes to get her way.

When I took a seat and was allowed to go into observer mode, that is when it all became real and the joy came rushing in like a flood. The music was pumping. The guests were dancing. Everyone was dancing because they could. The moment was tremendous and tangible proof of the power of the five steps of the Victory Dance.

I had invited Tom to the performance. He did not attend. Call me crazy, but I simply wanted to be able to share such a big moment with him. We had known each other so long and had been through so much. It still deeply hurt.

This time, however, I didn't let his absence steal my joy.

By the time I got home after 1 a.m., my mind was still firing on all cylinders. I lay in bed with eyes wide open well past 2 a.m., part from adrenaline, part from reflection, and part from the physical pain.

Even the perfectionist in me couldn't find much to criticize. We really did it. I had not exactly made up for losing my shot at a professional dance career more than twenty years earlier, but I proved that I did have the vision and ability to make things happen. I made the impossible possible.

I can still layout

With Dr. Palmer Bessey

Chita Rivera 'Woman of Valor'

On my own 'Red Carpet'

Victory Dancers flying

The Victory Dance Project Company

My Next Big Project

By 6 p.m. that Sunday, after two more weekend performances, the shows wrapped and everyone returned to life as usual. After a lovely dinner on the final night with Gary, my rehearsal director and partner in crime, and a few other friends, I went back to my apartment. I was alone, but I didn't feel lonely. I felt light and free.

It was time to choreograph something new for my life. Once one dance is complete, there is always another one ready to be created. No two dances will ever be the same—like life, the steps, ideas, concepts, and results of each dance will change with time and experience.

What was my new determination? First, I needed to get my health back in order. The production had taken its toll on my body and my diabetes. My shoulder was a wreck. My diet and exercise plans were nonexistent. When I got to my physical therapy appointment the following week my therapist looked at me standing crooked. "You are a hot mess," he remarked.

He was right. There was a lot of work to be done to unwind my battered body and lessen my pain and inflammation. That was fine with me—for the first time certainly since the accident, but really in my life, I let myself take some time and breathe.

I also redetermined to get back to my pursuit of a Madonna body. That nearly impossible standard was and is still lodged in my head, but I don't run from it anymore, because it keeps me focused on maintaining a healthy diet and regular training schedule.

I want to prove that even with type 1 diabetes, even with my ever-advancing age, and even with a severely deformed leg, I can be in phenomenal shape. It is a lofty goal, but as with anything great we want to achieve in life, the most rewarding things require tremendous effort.

The real question then becomes, "What am I really willing to do to get the results?" I was willing to do whatever it took and do the work, and this revelation uncovered my next big project—me!

I was in need of a full-body makeover, inside and out. I went back to my group fitness classes and got back in the pool. I also began my mornings by sitting on a bench in Riverside Park with my coffee. It was a joy to start every morning quietly sipping my coffee and reading. I challenged myself to stop rushing into the next activity for the sake of being busy. I cancelled trips to seminars and other appointments that would further drain my energy. I was exhausted and ready for a break.

It was time for Project Amy.

I Finally Understand

I learned a lot from the show about my limits, and I was grateful for the insight it provided. I also learned an unexpected financial lesson during that time. The woman I hired to find event sponsorship for the now-finished 2017 season had failed to do her job. I discovered this fact too late into production, and I ended up footing the majority of the production cost, including dancer payroll.

I have heard stories of people coming into money, but just a few short years later, they are broke. That was not going to be my story. I went through too much for that settlement, so I determined not to squander another dime. From that moment on, my money would used be for my needs and not for funding the work of the Victory Dance Project.

I talked with my financial advisor a few days after the performances wrapped.

"I finally understand," I told him.

While many people may react to sudden financial windfalls

by buying homes or cars or taking lavish trips, I had hired dancers and produced shows.

Maybe it was guilt. Maybe it was a sense of responsibility for having survived. Whatever the reason, I felt like I had gotten it out of my system. I was grateful for the wisdom to know I still needed to focus and transform this part of my life—and that I hadn't figured it out too late.

After my settlement had come in, the most surprising and disappointing moments came from those supposedly closest to me. I began to wonder whether people hung around because they cared or because they saw an opportunity. I still wonder this today. As a result, my radar is always up and my ear is listening for what isn't being said.

On the brighter and less cynical side, and despite my brief financial miscalculations, I had created a strong platform for myself in the process. I also employed a lot of young artists who were paid well for their time and talent. The dream of mine to pay artists their worth had come true.

I had been reading and spending time with a lot of successful people over the past year. One of the lessons I learned is that the best trainers, coaches, and mentors live their message rather than just speak it.

I decided it was time to live my message—to be excited about what was coming down the road for no other reason than because I could.

CHAPTER 23
Finding Enthusiasm in Everyday Life

AS MUCH AS I'D like to put a shiny bow on this final chapter and say that enthusiasm is our "big finale," I can't do that.

I'd also love to tell you that if you complete Steps One through Five of the Victory Dance, then the remainder of your days will be spent jumping up and down like Tom Cruise on Oprah's couch. Call me a cynic, but my idea of enthusiasm is a bit more subdued and realistic.

Life is peppered with changes, most of which we never saw coming, nor wanted to happen. One of my favorite quotes is by the brilliant and timeless Nora Ephron in her movie, *You've Got Mail*. Meg Ryan's character said, "People are always telling you that change is a good thing. All they are really saying is something you didn't want to happen has happened."

This is one of those lines that stuck with me over the years. Dr. Yaghoobzadeh, my dear cardiologist and friend, best summed me up by saying I am "cynically optimistic." He is spot on with this term. I can tell you from experience that looking down the barrel of yet another miscalculation or misfortune can be soul draining. My outward, sunny disposition always had everyone fooled into believing I could weather any storm. On the other hand, I secretly knew I was inches away from wishing for it all to simply end.

But I had one ingredient that seemed to keep it all together and help me take each labored step—and that is *resolve*. To me, enthusiasm and resolve are the two pieces that go together to make this step work.

Through a series of challenges and devastations, I have resolved to keep the joy in my life and continue to work to implement enthusiasm, even if at times it is compulsory. Through each painstaking reinvention, my forced smile that used to signify weakness in my eyes actually served an important purpose. My mantra has always been, "fake it 'til you make it." And damn, it looks like I actually made it!

One of the most important things I now realize is that determination is not always some earth-shattering proclamation. Have you ever determined to simply enjoy your coffee? How about resolving to have a better day than yesterday? Small determinations can be profoundly impactful.

My determination begins fresh each morning as I chant Nam Myoho Renge Kyo. I tell myself that today is going to be an amazing day and that the outcome might be even better than I could imagine.

Morning rituals are important to me. Whatever your morning ritual, does it ground you and help you focus for the day? Every day.

I don't mean to sound all kumbaya here, but stay with me for a minute.

To be completely honest, most days I still wake up in a panic. I seem to be hardwired to survive, but not to thrive. From the time I was diagnosed with type 1 diabetes as a little girl, my life has conditioned me to live in a continual state of fear, poised and ready for the other shoe to drop.

However, I am now racking up points on a new scorecard. I survived, which was the first miracle. I also built a tremendous company and am doing my own Victory Dance, literally this time! I have started cutting myself some slack. More importantly, I now actively endeavor to understand and experience "enthusiasm."

Now that I seek out and fully expect more out of my life, I am experiencing a surprising side effect—the "what if" floodgates are now wide open! WHAT IF everything worked out beyond my craziest imagination? WHAT IF I start asking for what I want and get a yes? WHAT IF I meet someone amazing and we fall in love?

Life is not all cupcakes and rainbows, but friends, hear me. Even when I literally could not move, I kept moving. And now, I'm here on the other side, living a life that I could have never imagined as a little girl who dreamed of being on stage with Broadway stars. It's not a dream anymore. It's my reality.

I kept dancing my way into finding the joy in every experience. Once I let go of trying to work toward happiness, I found I was already there!

Simple Disciplines

I have become a champion of the first four steps of the Victory Dance. Ironically, this last step requires the most focus. "Be the Master of your mind," writes Buddhist scholar Nichiren Daishonin. Simple words for a seemingly impossible task.

I don't know whether I can claim to be a master of my mind, but I can say that at each moment of great and unexpected or unwanted change, I took it on with great focus toward moving through the situation.

Whether it was growing up with a mentally ill mother, living with type 1 diabetes, losing my sight, giving up the car keys, getting pinned under the tire of a bus, having my heart broken, undergoing nearly sixty major surgeries, or begging for money from friends to buy food, it did not really matter in the end. No matter how far down life seemed to go, I never stopped moving. I was living my Victory Dance before I even knew what it was.

People have said to me again recently, "When is enough going to be enough? Do you really need to set your expectations so high?" For me enough is never enough. I am in the game to see how far I can go. I like to push the mark.

I am also learning not to take life so seriously. I frequently hear myself saying, "I am not in a burn ICU or cardiac trauma unit, so how serious can this really be?" Perspective, please.

This is great reminder to continue to build my happiness muscles for Step Five. It's also a reminder to stay in the present moment. I know that might sound like a New Age philosophy to some, but to me it is a charge to slow down and enjoy a life that is absolutely racing by at a frantic pace.

One of my new goals is to feel excited every day. It is a challenge, but I am working to redirect my mindset to be excited about any and all tasks in front of me. When I speak to audiences, I talk a lot about simple disciplines. Starting small is often the best solution—do a new task for thirty minutes, exercise fifteen minutes rather than none, or eat a few more vegetables and a little less bread.

Small steps, taken often enough, will ultimately lead to a bigger win.

After the accident, I remember feeling that I would never be out of a wheelchair. My first days and months trying to learn to walk again were grueling, but I took it one step and one leg lift at a time.

I kept up the simple disciplines, and in six months I was up and moving and eventually off a walker. Some days I could do more than others—and this is also true today. The difference is that I judge and criticize myself less than before.

As a woman facing difficult health situations on a daily basis I take pride in the amount of time and energy I put into managing my diabetes and maintaining my rehabilitation. It is tough every single day. Some days, it's an hourly battle.

Does all the effort and vigilance annoy me? Of course it does! I am human after all. But the end result is a beautiful dance that you can look at and say, "I built this. I did my steps and look what resulted!"

Any situation, any obstacle can be transformed into something of value, no matter how devastating. Those are not empty words. I am living and breathing proof. This is excitement—showing up every day and doing you. Whatever your challenge, I congratulate you for taking on the first steps. **In just trying you have already WON.**

Right Where You Are

Every once in a while, people like to ask me questions like:

"What do you think your life would be like if you hadn't had the accident?"

"Do you think you would have taken the same path?"

"Do you wish it never happened?"

Such questions serve no purpose. This other mythical path that my life didn't take is irrelevant. The fact is it did happen. I've spent untold hours replaying the events of May 1, 2009, but I cannot change the facts.

What I can change is how I react and how I choose every day to work with my situation.

That's what these steps are all about.

Today, I look forward to the simple things. I get excited about my early morning coffee and sitting in Riverside Park for some quiet reading time. I get excited to have time to train and eat well. To me, enthusiasm is about greeting life every day with a sense of grace and understanding.

My natural tendency is to live for the accolades or the next big moment.

My goal now is to live in the middle.

I don't want to live in the past. I don't want to spend all of my energy chasing a big future. I want to find the joy right where I'm standing (and in the fact that I can still stand at all).

The takeaway here is not, "Dream small and be content with what you have now." Far from it! I am still working toward creating more earth-shattering, bold moments. I also know I am alive for a reason. I want to continue to reach for big things with a heart of gratitude for every experience, big and small. This is a relatively new revelation for me due to the lifetime I spent waiting for my "sickness" to get the best of me.

I think often of the vow I made on the day of my mediation. I feel a tremendous sense of purpose to inspire and motivate others in creating their Victory Dance.

Each step brings with it its own unique challenges. Step Five is no exception. If you are waiting to "reach" happiness, be prepared to wait for a lifetime. To have enthusiasm truly means that in *whatever* is going on in life, there exists the potential to see and feel joy.

I am not happy that a bus hit me. I am, however, completely ecstatic about the direction I have willed my life to go since that moment.

Has it changed my life? Absolutely.

Am I continuing to move ahead and create value? I certainly am.

My life is far from perfect. Every day I have to remind myself to live my message. Some days I'm admittedly better at it than others. I still struggle, but every day I make sure to do a Victory Dance. And by now, you should know why—because I can!

EPILOGUE
The Closing Curtain

TODAY IS THURSDAY, SEPTEMBER 14, 2017. It is warm and muggy in New York City. I am perched in my reclining chair with my laptop on my lap. Madonna is playing on Spotify (who else?).

As I examine my present state of being, I recognize some things that I cannot change: I still have diabetes, I am still visually impaired, I still have a mangled leg, and I am still single (but determined to do something about that one).

What is changing is my perspective. I feel so much less fear. The blank canvas that is my life is exciting. I appreciate that I can step back from the frantic pace of survival from years past and take time to rest and be still.

Like so many others, I am concerned about the discourse and divide in the world. I have written this book as a guidepost for finding and feeling more joy. It does not mean that life will be free of obstacles, challenges, or defeats. What it does mean is that there is a roadmap to navigate this crazy thing we call life.

I am not a victim of circumstance, and neither are you. You have such a unique mission. So take a moment right now and ask yourself some tough but revealing questions such as:

- What does my Victory Dance look and feel like?
- How will I know when I'm living it?
- Where am I in the process?
- Do I need to rework some steps so they have a better flow?
- Am I excited about at least one aspect of my life?

Wherever you are, I say congratulations to you! Taking on this process is itself courage and resolve. As I say to every audience to whom I speak, please do me a favor and just:

Dance Because You Can!

Transforming Trauma into Triumph with The Five Steps

I must give you a HUGE congratulations yet again. It takes true courage and self- love to want to transform life's adversities. I am so proud of you.

Here is a recap guide.

Step One: Determination

Who is determining your outcomes? Is it you or your Dr. Know-It-All?

What determination can you make NOW toward your victory? You don't have to know the how. Just determine the end result and work backward from there. The action steps will become clear.

Step Two: Acceptance.

Let me reiterate a prime point: accepting a difficult situation does not mean you have to LIKE it. It does mean we need to accept our present circumstance so we can make moves toward improving it.

With acceptance comes clarity.

Step Three: Never Give Up

No matter how bad things seem or how impassible an obstacle you are facing, know this: keep moving. Take one action a day. Apply the idea of simple disciplines. Over time the situation is likely to resolve or improve.

Take extra great care of yourself. Often in this crazy-paced world we forget to stop and breath. What small thing can you do today that is just for YOU?

Step Four: Courage

Just picking up this book and delving into this process takes courage. Despite anxiety or fear the willingness to keep moving is courage.

Give yourself credit for what your ARE accomplishing everyday. You are amazing.

Step Five: Enthusiasm

What brings you joy? How can you feel happy and content even in the midst of life's ups and downs?

How can you implement a simpler and more attainable idea of enthusiasm?

Most importantly always:

Dance Because You Can!

I want to hear from YOU. What is working or not working. How is your life growing and changing?

Keep in touch.

Join our world at www.amyjordanspeaks.com for free videos, coaching insights and workouts!

Author Bio

Amy Jordan lives her mantra: 'Dance Because You Can.'

Amy encompasses a very optimistic spirit and while wearing many hats, she has been able to bring them all together. Her professional knowledge and personal experiences have given her the insight needed to inspire others. She is a motivational speaker, coach, fitness expert and first and foremost a dancer!

Amy's dance life includes study with choreographers for Madonna, Michael Jackson and Paula Abdul. The Victory Dance Project, Amy's professional dance company members credits include Broadway shows The Lion King, Hamilton and Chicago as well a Rockette and company members from The Alvin Ailey American Dance Theater and Dance Theater of Harlem. Amy's SWEET ENUFF Movement is an award winning youth diabetes and obesity prevention program. SWEET ENUFF was a top 5 national finalist of First Lady Michelle Obama's 'End Childhood Obesity Challenge.'

Amy has Type 1 Juvenile Diabetes and fought most of her life to hide her chronic condition. Life challenged Amy again when she was hit and run over by a New York City bus. The accident nearly ended her life and her leg came close to being amputated.

Amy Jordan is on a mission motivating and inspiring others to overcome ANY adversity. She tells everyone she meets, 'Please Dance Because You Can.'

Amy shares her unique D.A.N.C.E. philosophy in her signature presentation 'Dance Because You Can.' She believes that always focusing on Creating Your Own Victory Dance is the key to success in business, leadership and life!

Amy Jordan regularly speaks for a variety of audiences (ranging from entry level to experienced executives) for corporations, business groups, associations, colleges, universities, youth groups and sports organizations.

Any organization looking for an inspirational speaker, who will inspire and motivate their audience to overcome adversity and achieve greater success, needs to book Amy for a keynote and/or workshop training. She speaks to groups from 20-20,000+.

www.amyjordanspeaks.com
Contact Amy Jordan: win@amyjordanspeaks.com

Resources:
New York Presbyterian Weill Cornell Medical Center: www.nyp.org
Hospital for Special Surgery: www.hss.edu
SGI-USA: www.sgi-usa.org

Cover design: Untamed Media
Cover Photo: Brian Thomas
Additional Photos: Christopher Duggan, Jordan Hiraldo, Ramon Morillo, Brian Thomas, Cherylynn Tsushima, Val Westover.

CPSIA information can be obtained
at www.ICGtesting.com
Printed in the USA
BVHW091147250922
647877BV00003B/23

9 781478 798859